THE COMPLETE GUIDE TO THE SHAR-PEI

Vanessa Richie

Publication Data

Vanessa Richie

The Complete Guide to the Shar-Pei ---- First edition.

Summary: "Successfully raising a Shar-Pei from puppy to old age" --- Provided by publisher.

ISBN: 978-1-952069-75-8

[1.Shar Pei --- Non-Fiction] I. Title.

Design by Sorin Rădulescu

First paperback edition, 2020

TABLE OF CONTENTS

CHAPTER 17

The Aging Shar-Pei

INTRODUCTION

Photo Courtesy of Cortney Petrillo

The Shar-Pei may not be a highly popular breed, but it is still among the most easily recognizable. Once you have learned what a Shar-Pei looks like, it really isn't a breed you will recognize as being anything other than what it is. The wrinkly face comes with a very short, square jaw line that is often described as being like a hippo's. The wrinkles tend to cover the shoulders and legs and make the dogs look older and wiser than other breeds.

Shar-Pei are among the oldest breeds in the world. With their roots in China, Shar-Pei were raised to hunt, herd, and fight. As their purpose shifted to being more of a companion, the breed's numbers began to wane, with fewer people being able to purchase and tend to the dogs. At one point, their population declined to the point of near extinction. Then they made their way out of China, and there was a booming interest in the unique-looking breed. Besides those adorable wrinkles, another distinctive feature is a blue-black tongue.

The Shar-Pei is an amazingly loyal and loving dog, but also intelligent and opinionated. They tend to want to be with their people, but they also like to have things their own way. They can be very stubborn, which makes them a bad fit for people who have little to no experience with training dogs. They require a firm, consistent hand in their training. However, for dog parents who know how to train them, Shar-Pei are a great breed to have in the home.

They require a bit of extra grooming because of their wrinkles, but with short, bristly fur, Shar-Pei coats do not require much in the way of brushing or bathing.

You can usually hear Shar-Pei breathing, especially when they are sleeping. They are also very messy drinkers and eaters. They do not handle heat well, so you have to make sure to keep them cool.

The breed does not like strangers and has a strong prey drive because of its hunting background. If you are a sociable person who likes to have people over to visit often, this probably isn't the right breed for you.

The Shar-Pei is a great family member for the right home. It is an ancient breed that can be affectionate and playful around the family.

*Photo Courtesy
of Lorna Bleming*

CHAPTER 1
The Unique History Of The Shar-Pei

Even though Shar-Pei are considered one of the oldest known dog breeds, it isn't known exactly how much of the dog's history is actually history and how much is legend. Based on scientific studies, it is thought that the breed has been largely unchanged for about 2,000 years.

Origins Of The Name – A Physical Description

A quick look at the Shar-Pei can leave the impression that the shiny coat is silky and smooth. However, the name Shar-Pei translates to "sand skin" because that silky-looking coat is quite coarse. Since the fur is short and rough, it is incredibly easy to groom. However, the wrinkles require extra care to ensure that there aren't any infections hiding in the folds.

The wrinkles were intentionally bred because Shar-Pei were largely used as guard dogs for royal families and nobles, as well as for sport. Their aggressive nature made them ideal fighting dogs, and their large hippo-like jowls made them very effective once they latched onto their opponent. The wrinkles made it hard for an opponent to hold onto them.

Potential Origins

It is thought that the first Shar-Pei originated around 200 BCE. However, the first documented evidence of them was in northern India during the 18th century. They definitely originated from China, though their history before the 18th century is unknown. From the description, the breed was very similar to the Shar-Pei of today.

Photo Courtesy of Charlemagne Fezza

The history of the breed isn't well recorded likely because of the upheaval in China during the 20th century. During this time the breed was in sharp decline and nearly went extinct.

Near Extinction – How They Were Saved

What little is known about the Shar-Pei's history includes the belief that the original dogs were fiercely loyal and could perform numerous types of work as needed to help peasants to survive daily life. It is believed that the breed originated in the southern provinces of China. Over time, the rulers saw the dogs and decided to use them as protectors.

When World War II started, China was already in the midst of a civil war between two different Communist parties. Following the end of World War II, the civil war resumed. The resolution to that civil war was the beginning of the current Chinese government, and that government was against everything that was a reminder of the elite Chinese who had ruled the country for millennia. In a bid to completely remove evidence of the existence of the ruling class, all historical

FUN FACT
Ancient Breed

The Shar-Pei has been around since at least 200 BC. Archeologists have found statues resembling the breed in China dating to that time. It's thought that the breed originated in the area around the village of Tai Li.

Photo Courtesy
of Shawn Pucknell

documents and reminders were destroyed, including dog breeds that were associated with them. This unfortunately included the Shar-Pei. Long before the rise of the Communist party, China was a fairly closed country. The culture had not spread extensively, so when the Shar-Pei breed became endangered, there were no others of the breed outside of India. As a result, by the middle of the 20th century, the breed was nearly extinct. Then the side that lost the civil war fled to Hong Kong and Taiwan, including a few breeders who took some Shar-Pei with them.

Photo Courtesy of Kaydia Davis

During the 1960s, the US began to create its own documentation of the breed. By the middle of the 1970s, Americans began wanting to have their own Shar-Pei. Shar-Pei breeder Matgo Law, who lived in Hong Kong, saw this as an opportunity to help bring the dog back from the brink of extinction by playing on the sudden interest.

The Shar-Pei Today

Today, Shar-Pei are no longer on the verge of extinction. However, the period when they were on the brink led to their health becoming somewhat compromised. Some breeders took to using less reputable breeding practices, and with a breed as old as the Shar-Pei, there were already a number of health concerns.

The American Kennel Club recognized the breed in 1992, making it the 134th breed to be recognized by the organization. The Chow Chow, another Chinese breed that has the same black tongue, is thought to be about the same age, and potentially related to the Shar-Pei.

Photo Courtesy
of Sue Hague

The following are thought to be the oldest dog breeds that have changed little over several thousand years:

- Chow Chow, going back as far as 200 BCE

- Shar-Pei, going back to an estimated year of 206 BCE

- Saluki, an Egyptian breed that goes back to around 330 BCE

- Samoyed, a Siberian breed thought to go back to 1000 BCE

- Alaskan Malamute, an Alaskan breed thought to go back to 1000 BCE

- Afghan Hound, a breed from Afghanistan, thought to go back to 6000 BCE

- Basenji, from central Africa, thought to go back to roughly 6000 BCE

- Akita Inu, a Japanese breed with a history that goes so far back its origins are unknown

The Shar-Pei shares a lot in common with these other ancient breeds, including a history that is largely unknown. Many of these breeds were integral to the people in their region of origin – so much so that we associate them with their geographic areas of origin. They all have a distinct appearance that shows what kinds of jobs they performed in the places where they lived, and the Shar-Pei is no different. Their loyal, loving nature with their family is a reflection of just how close the breed has been with people. Though they can be aggressive, a family that knows how to patiently train them can have a fantastic dog with a long history of being a great companion and family member.

CHAPTER 2
A Unique Look For A Loyal Guardian

The long history of Shar-Pei as companions has made them fiercely loyal to their people. Even though they look cute, they are absolutely not the right dog for someone who has never had a dog or who doesn't have experience in training dogs. Like German Shepherds and Chow Chows, Shar-Pei have a history as protectors, which makes them potentially dangerous. All intelligent breeds require a firm training regimen, but dogs with a history of protecting are particularly dangerous to bring into the home because they require someone to be the alpha. If they cannot quickly identify an alpha, Shar-Pei will consider themselves in charge of the home.

That said, if you know how to be firm and consistent, showing respect while making sure your dog knows his place, you won't find many breeds that are as wonderful to have in the home.

Photo Courtesy of Laur Dyck

Their distinctive look is what really makes people interested in bringing a Shar-Pei into their lives. The wrinkles make them look wise, and their adorable faces look like they are ready to just lie down to cuddle with you. They are more likely to show their guardian side when you have company or when out walking in an unfamiliar area. They want to keep you safe, so they are suspicious of people they don't know. With their family though, Shar-Pei are serene and loving, though they can be fairly independent when the mood strikes them. Early socialization and training will make them much more accepting of strangers and is very important.

*Photo Courtesy
of Erika Sinner
IG @crazy4pei*

The Defining Physical Characteristics Of The Shar-Pei

Once you see a Shar-Pei, you will never forget it, especially if you see one as a puppy. They appear to be a mass of wrinkles as puppies, but they eventually grow into their skin. By the time they are adults, the wrinkles are primarily around the face and shoulders, something that breeders have worked to achieve over the years. All dogs with wrinkles require extra care since wrinkles capture dirt in the folds, which can result in an infection.

Shar-Pei tend to shed a lot but don't tend to make much of a mess. The short coat requires very little grooming. The coat colors are:

- Black
- Cream
- Chocolate
- Red
- Blue

There are some dogs that appear to have patterns, such as brindles and spots, but they aren't considered to be purebred Shar-Pei.

Another distinctive feature is their black tongue, which you will see often because they spend a lot of time panting. They are a brachial dog,

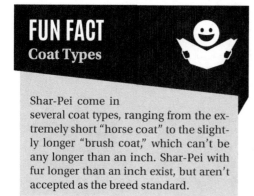

FUN FACT
Coat Types

Shar-Pei come in several coat types, ranging from the extremely short "horse coat" to the slightly longer "brush coat," which can't be any longer than an inch. Shar-Pei with fur longer than an inch exist, but aren't accepted as the breed standard.

meaning they have flat faces. This can make breathing difficult. Their mouths are often compared to hippo mouths because they have a similar rectangular shape, which made them so effective when fighting. Their mouths are always well padded by all of the wrinkles, which can hide the unique shape until you throw food their way.

Their adorable face is capped by a pair of small, triangular ears that stand out on that wrinkly face. It helps give them an inquisitive look when their ears are standing up.

Shar-Pei stand at about 20 inches tall and weigh between 45 and 60 pounds, making them a large dog. They are solidly built, so you will be able to see their muscles under that coarse fur.

Photo Courtesy of Jerad Cook

Photo Courtesy of Pamela Tatam

Health Problems Common To Shar-Pei

Most Shar-Pei today come from those few dogs that were brought out of China. This means that any health problems have been passed down through the generations. With the boom in breeding during the late 1970s and all through the 1980s, those health problems were exacerbated.

A Breed With Many Potential Health Issues

Irresponsible breeding for the better part of two decades has caused problems to be passed on to Shar-Pei puppies at a more rapid pace than likely would have been possible with other breeds that had a higher population. This is why it is particularly important to be careful about which puppy you adopt – you could end up with a puppy that has many health issues and a bad temperament.

There are some issues that are fairly rare and very specific to the breed because of those low breeding numbers. Diseases are highlighted here, and more details about symptoms and treatments are covered in Chapter 16.

Swollen Hock Syndrome is a genetic disease that causes the dog's body to be unable to break down amyloid protein. As the protein accumulates, it can damage the kidneys and liver. This disorder is deadly and dogs with it usually die young.

Photo Courtesy of Carla Darling

Shar-Pei have several problems around their face. The small ears are prone to infection, in part because of the wrinkles, and require regular cleaning. The additional padding on their lips can become a problem, getting in the way when the dogs are eating. The wrinkles on their face are also prone to infection.

Shar-Pei may suffer from rashes that cause an area of skin to become inflamed, causing the fur to fall out. They may also suffer from mucinosis, which are bumps that appear on the skin. Sometimes the bumps can discharge mucus. Neither of these conditions are deadly, but they could be uncomfortable and irritating to your dog.

FUN FACT
Wrinkles with a Purpose

Shar-Pei were bred to guard the royal family, and their wrinkles were designed to help protect them in dogfights. The other dog would get a mouth full of skin, and the Shar-Pei's internal organs would be protected.

Rectal prolapse can be deadly, and it is often confused with anal abscesses. If you notice your dog has a protruding mass around his rectum, you need to get the dog to the vet as quickly as possible.

Shar-Pei are also more likely to have an immune deficiency than most other breeds. The puppies are more likely to suffer from it, and some can outgrow the problem.

A Warning About Brachial Dogs

All brachial dogs have breathing issues. Brachial dogs have short snouts, which is what tends to make breathing difficult for them. They are prone to overheating because dogs cool off through their mouths. With their air passages already restricted because of their short noses, they cannot properly cool off in the summer. This means you have to exercise brachial dogs during the cool parts of the day, particularly during the summer.

The short snout also tends to make Shar-Pei louder than most other dogs. You can usually hear them coming, they tend to make a mess when they drink, and they snore. You should be aware of how noisy they can be since this can be surprising at first.

Strong-Willed, Independent, And Potentially Aggressive

"The Shar-Pei are a quiet dog by nature, but can be territorial. It is important to understand the disposition and engage your puppy with proper socialization and set boundaries."

Sheila Marquart
Tuck 'N Roll Acres

Photo Courtesy
ᴀirah Dipatuan & Raymond Lopez

Like most guard dogs, the Shar-Pei is a very strong-willed breed that can be aggressive when not properly trained. They usually don't like strangers, so they are known for being aloof. They are more openly hostile to other animals. They are also incredibly intelligent, which makes them easy to train when it is done early. This is a breed that has been bred for protection over many centuries. This means that they are quite loving with the people they know, but can be very wary of strangers. To keep them from being a problem, Shar-Pei require early socialization with both other dogs and people. Without a complete approach to socialization, you may find that you won't be able to take your dog out on hikes or other forms of exercise because of their protective tendencies.

Having a Shar-Pei that is wary is very different from having a Shar-Pei that is aggressive. That natural assertive confidence and alertness can be used to ensure you can enjoy outings as long as you have taught your dog that most strangers can be ignored.

If not properly trained, Shar-Pei may get overexcited, running around the home and knocking people over. And, at their size, they can do some serious damage. When it is time to relax, Shar-Pei are more than happy to flop down near you and simply enjoy being near the family.

Not Interested In Play

Shar-Pei aren't particularly playful. If you enjoy hiking and being outdoors, they can be great companions – though you should not jog with them. They do not do well with vigorous exercise because of their short snouts. They are perfectly content to hike with you and explore. However, at home, they will be much more likely to prefer lounging in the room with you to playing.

They do enjoy training when they understand that you are in charge. They like to do something with an obvious purpose, and playing doesn't seem to qualify. Chapter 13 provides details about how you can play with your Shar-Pei, and it involves more work on your part then simply buying a ball and throwing it.

If you prefer to just lounge around your home, your Shar-Pei will appreciate that and will be more than happy to just be lazy near you. Typically, they aren't big cuddlers – at least they won't try to be your lap dog since they are clearly too big for that role.

CHAPTER 3
Finding Your Shar-Pei

"Shar-pei are unique in that no two are alike in look or behavior. It is one of the few (if only) breed within the AKC that carries such diversity. Potential new owners should first educate themselves regarding the breed and its potential health issues. Talk to several owners and breeders about their experiences. Visit in person to see the pups' parents and other relatives if possible, as all puppies will be a representative of their heritage. A quality breeder will be upfront about the pros and cons of their bloodlines, and have no problem providing references."

Debbie Raynor
DC Shar-pei

Photo Courtesy of June Juul Nielsen

Deciding that the Shar-Pei is the right dog for you is only the first step in the exciting journey to adopt your next family member. Once you know you want a Shar-Pei, you have to decide if you want a puppy or an adult dog – there are benefits and drawbacks to both ages. Ultimately, it's about what kind of training you want to do.

Considerations And Steps To Rescue An Adult Shar-Pei

How much work can you manage? Will you be able to deal with an excitable puppy that has everything to learn? Or do you prefer an adult that may have problems that you have to help the dog work through? Puppies are almost always more work, but you never know what kind of experience an adult dog has been through which will affect how he reacts to the world around him. With a breed like the Shar-Pei, you need to be careful about adopting an adult because if the adult hasn't been properly trained, it can be a real struggle to train the dog. Adult Shar-Pei are usually not a good fit for families with children, especially young children.

The hunt to find your newest family member is going to take a while. Because of Shar-Pei's strength and power, you will need to spend time fixing up your home to prepare for your new family member. Furthermore, to ensure that you get a healthy puppy that will be your loving companion for as long as possible, you'll need to find a reputable breeder who cares more about the puppies than money.

The approach to adopting an adult Shar-Pei is the same as it is for adopting a puppy from a breeder. However, with such an intelligent dog, you will want to ask a lot more questions about adopting an adult, particularly inquiring about the dog's previous experiences.

Considerations

Rescuing any dog comes with some inherent risks. While it is possible to find Shar-Pei puppies at dog rescue groups, it is much more likely that you will find a rescued adult. Adopting an older Shar-Pei could require a lot of work, and knowing the dog's history is incredibly important so you know what to expect. Since the dogs can be stubborn, people may give up on a Shar-Pei without putting much effort into training the dog.

Think about the following to determine if an adult Shar-Pei is a good fit for your home.

Photo Courtesy
of Jerad Cook

- **Why do you want to bring an adult into your home? What are your expectations for the dog?**

- **Shar-Pei understand the commands you are giving, but they may be particularly stubborn if they haven't been properly trained. Do you have the patience to work through the issues that an adult may have?**

Rescue organizations collect as much information as they can about the dogs they rescue, but their knowledge of a dog's history is usually very limited. The benefits of rescuing a Shar-Pei are very similar to adopting any rescue dog, though you do need to be more careful in case a dog has not been properly trained and socialized. You need to know about the dog's temperament so you can start planning how to help him to overcome past experiences. The odds are very good that you aren't going to be starting from scratch with housetraining. Adult dogs are awake more often than puppies and, while it may take them a bit longer to warm up to you, you can bond much faster with an adult, depending on its age.

An adult Shar-Pei may be a bit more wary, especially if he was not socialized or was previously treated poorly. Many rescue sites will be more wary of adopting out adult dogs with obvious temperament or personality issues as they can be dangerous. Shar-Pei's natural suspicion toward strangers will make them wary of you and your family – and you should not adopt an adult if you have young children unless the dog's history with young children is known to be positive. Similarly, you will need to be very careful about adopting a Shar-Pei if you have other pets at home. Once your adult dog bonds with you and your family though, it will be like flipping an affection switch, and then you really could not ask for a more loyal and calm dog.

- **Are you able to properly dog-proof your home before the dog arrives?**

You can't simply bring an adult dog into your home and let him run around unchecked. As with a puppy, you will need to have a dedicated space for your new dog to make sure he learns the rules before being allowed to roam the home. In the beginning you will need a space for the dog to become familiar with you and your home as you assess your new Shar-Pei's personality and capabilities. It is a fairly important consideration, particularly if you have other dogs and cats, as you will want to ensure harmony in your home.

- **Do you have pets who will be affected by a new dog?**

Photo Courtesy of Cielo Phillips

Shar-Pei are more aggressive toward other dogs and animals than toward people. If a dog's history with other pets is not known, it is probably best not to select that particular dog unless you can ensure a slow, careful introduction to your own pets over a month or so. You will need to introduce them on neutral territory, which will give you a good idea of how well the Shar-Pei will do with your current dogs, but you will still need to keep them apart for longer than most other breeds to ensure that your new Shar-Pei understands that the dogs are also part of the pack, and not a threat to him.

You will need to be careful about how your other dogs react as well. Shar-Pei are very bossy, so if you already have an alpha dog, it can be difficult to teach them to get along. Even if your current dogs are very friendly, you will still want to be careful when introducing them and then letting them interact in your home.

You may not be able to get a complete health record for an adult Shar-Pei, but it is likely that you will find a dog that has already been spayed or neutered, as well as chipped. Unless you adopt a Shar-Pei that has health issues (these should be disclosed by the rescue organization if available), rescues tend to be less costly at the first vet visit than puppies – for the first few years it's likely you won't pay nearly as much to take care of your Shar-Pei's health. You will be spending a lot more time training though. Puppies have a short attention span, which equates to many short training sessions. Adults require more attention and longer durations of training so that they get accustomed to listening to you. This dedicated attention is good not only for teaching the rules of the home, but for bonding with the dog.

Older dogs give you more immediate gratification. You don't have to go through the sleepless nights that come with a new puppy or the frustration of housetraining.

Finally, one of the biggest benefits of getting an adult dog is that it will already be full size. You don't have to guess the size, making it far easier to get the right gear and dog supplies in the beginning.

If you want to rescue a Shar-Pei, you can start with one of these two sites:

- Pei People Shar-Pei Rescue - http://www.peipeople.com/

- North American Shar-Pei Rescue - http://www.sharpeirescue.com/

If you prefer to rescue a Shar-Pei from a breeder, they will have a more comprehensive understanding of the dog you are rescuing. Contracts and guarantees are meant as much to protect the puppies as to protect the families who adopt them. If you want an adult, consider calling breeders to see if they have any adults available. You will need to ask them a different set of questions than if you were adopting a puppy, but they will be able to provide you with a lot of details about the dog, his personality, and if there are any potential issues.

Rescuing A Shar-Pei

If you are interested in adopting from a rescue organization or group, there are several things to keep in mind. This section covers the questions you should ask. If you are considering adopting a puppy from a rescue group instead of a breeder, ask the same questions.

To get a better idea of the rescue organization and how much they know about the dogs they adopt out, ask the following questions.

- What was the reason the dog was surrendered?
- Did the dog have any health issues when he arrived?
- Do they know how the dog was treated by the previous family (including what kind of training the dog has had, if he was mistreated, or if he was socialized)?
- How many homes do they know the dog has been in?
- What kind of vet care has the dog had? Do they have records from before the dog arrived into their care?
- Will the dog require extra medical attention based on known or suspected problems?
- Is the dog housetrained?
- How well does the dog react to strangers and walks in familiar areas?
- Does the dog have good eating habits? Does he tend to be more aggressive when eating?
- How does the dog react to children and other pets?
- Are there any known allergies?
- Does the dog have any known additional dietary restrictions?
- Is there a trial period or home visit prior to the adoption?
- Will the organization take the dog back if there are problems after adoption?

Rescue groups should have at least a basic understanding of how well a Shar-Pei interacts with other dogs. For breeders, there is a benefit because the adult rescues are already living with other dogs, so they have a certain amount of socialization already completed.

Once you have identified a dog you would like to adopt, you will want to meet the dog before the final adoption. Some places will bring the dog to your home, others will have you come into the facility to meet the Shar-Pei. Given the personality of the dog, you definitely need to meet your Shar-Pei before you make the adoption. Some places will even allow for a trial period so that you can determine if the dog is a good fit for your home and situations before you make that final commitment. Every rescue has a different adoption process, so you will want to understand that first interaction, who needs to be present (just you, all of the adults in your home, the whole family, or some other combination of people in your home).

Considerations For Adopting A Puppy And Picking A Breeder

Puppies are a major time investment, and a dog as intelligent and stubborn as the Shar-Pei will make some aspects of raising a puppy that much harder. However, a puppy can be a better fit in your home if you make sure to put in dedicated time to training and socializing. If you have pets at home, a puppy is definitely better than an adult (unless you can find out if the adult is already well socialized).

Think about the following to determine if a Shar-Pei puppy is a good fit for your home.

- **How much time do you have available? Are you willing to give up all of your free time and to work your schedule around your puppy?**

One of the biggest considerations is how much time you are willing to invest. All puppies are a lot of work, starting with the moment the puppy enters your care. While the Shar-Pei's temperament is largely predictable, how you train and socialize your puppy will affect nearly every aspect of the dog's adult life. Training and socializing can take up a large chunk of time in the early days, but they are absolutely essential for raising a healthy Shar-Pei.

You also want the puppy to know that your home is safe and that everyone has the puppy's best interest in mind. This can be exhausting because the dogs have energy from an early age. Without proper training and socialization, you may have a dog that is destructive and disregarding of your at-

Photo Courtesy
of Marie Collins

tempts to train him. It does take a firm, consistent hand to train a breed like the Shar-Pei, so the time investment is much greater than it is with many other breeds.

- **Are you able to be firm and consistent with such an adorable puppy?**

From the very beginning, you have to establish yourself and your family as the ones in charge so that your Shar-Pei understands the hierarchy from the moment he enters your home. You will need to be prepared to be patient and consistent, no matter how frustrated you are or how cute those puppy eyes are.

- **Do you have the time, energy, and budget to puppy-proof your home?**

The work to prepare your home for your puppy's arrival begins long before your puppy arrives though. Puppy-proofing the home is as time-consuming as childproofing your home. If you do not have the time to puppy-proof your home, then you should consider getting an adult dog. Chapter 5 provides details about the specific things you should do to prepare your home before bringing a Shar-Pei into it.

On the plus side, you will have more time with a puppy than with an adult. You will have records about the puppy and the puppy's parents, making it easier to identify the potential problems your Shar-Pei may suffer. This makes it considerably easier to ensure your puppy stays healthy and to catch potential issues earlier.

Some people find it easier to bond with puppies than with adult dogs. A young puppy will be nervous in a new home, but most adjust quickly because they are predisposed to enjoying the company of those around them. Your primary job will be protecting your puppy and making sure that you patiently train him. We will cover this more in a later chapter.

Finding a responsible breeder is the best thing you can do for your puppy since good breeders work with only healthy parents, reducing the odds that a puppy will have serious health issues. Always take the time to research breeders. Although breeders for Shar-Pei are largely reputable, that doesn't mean there won't be some who are more interested in earning a lot of money than in caring for their dogs.

FUN FACT
Once-Rare Breed

In the 1960s and 70s, Shar-Pei nearly went extinct thanks to hefty taxes on dogs in China. In the 1970s, a Shar-Pei breeder named Matgo Law, who lived in Hong Kong, pleaded with the world to save the breed. Life magazine published an issue with a Shar-Pei on the cover, and puppy sales skyrocketed in the United States. Now, the breed no longer holds a spot in the Guinness World Records as the world's rarest dog.

Choosing A Breeder

Once you understand enough about the breed to know what you are getting into, it is time to start talking to breeders. The goal is to determine which breeders are willing to take the time to patiently and thoroughly answer all of your questions. They should have as much love for their Shar-Pei as they want you to feel for your new puppy. And they should want to make sure that their puppies go to good homes. If you are in the US, you can start looking for breeders near you from the American Kennel Club recommendations.

If you find someone who posts regular pictures and information about the parents and the progress of the mother's pregnancy and vet visits, that is a very good sign. The best breeders will not only talk about their dogs and the plans for the parents in the future, they will stay in contact with you after you take the puppy home and answer any questions as they arise. These are the kinds of breeders who are likely to have waiting lists. The active interest in knowing about what happens to the puppies later shows that they care a great deal about each individual dog. You also want to find a breeder who is willing to talk about the potential problems with Shar-Pei. Good breeders will want to ensure the family adopting one of their puppies is capable of properly socializing and training a Shar-Pei. Both of these activities are essential as a puppy matures.

It is likely that for each breeder you call the conversation will last about an hour. If a breeder does not have time to talk and isn't willing to talk with you later, you can cross them off your list. After you have talked with each possible breeder, compare answers.

The following are some questions to ask prospective breeders:

- Ask if you can visit in person. The answer should always be yes, and if it isn't, you don't need to ask anything further. Thank the breeder and hang up. Even if the breeder is located in a different state, they should allow you to visit the facility.

- Ask about the required health tests and certifications a breeder has for their puppies. These points are detailed further in the next section, so make sure to check off the available tests and certifications for each breeder. If they don't have all of the tests and certifications, you may want to remove the breeder from consideration.

- Make sure that the breeder always takes care of all of the initial health requirements in the first few weeks through the early months, particularly shots. Puppies require that certain procedures be done before they leave their mother to ensure they are healthy. Vaccinations and worming typically start around six weeks after the puppies are born, then need to be continued every three weeks. By the time your puppy is old enough to come home, he should be well into the procedures, or even completely through with the first phases of these important health care needs.

- Ask if the puppy is required to be spayed or neutered before reaching a certain age of maturity. Typically, these procedures are done in the puppies' best interest.

- Find out if the breeder is part of a Shar-Pei organization or group.

- Ask about the first phases of your puppy's life, such as how the breeder plans to care for the puppy during those first few months. They should be able to provide a lot of detail, and they should do this without sounding as though they are irritated that you want to know. They should also let you know how much training you can expect to be done prior to the puppy's arrival in your home. It is possible that the breeder may start housetraining the puppy. If so, ask how quickly the puppy has picked up on the training. You want to be able to pick up from where the breeder left off once your Shar-Pei reaches your home.

- Ask what kind of advice the breeder gives about raising your Shar-Pei puppy. They should be more than happy to help guide you to doing what is best for your dog because they will want the puppies to live happy, healthy lives. You should also be able to rely on a breeder's recommendations, advice, and additional care after the puppy arrives at your home. Basically, you are getting customer support, as well as a great chance of having a healthy dog.

- Ask how many breeds the breeder manages a year. How many sets of parents does the breeder have? Puppies can take a lot of time and attention, and the mother should have some downtime between pregnancies. Learn about the breeder's standard operations to find out if they are taking care of the parents and treating them like valuable family members and not strictly as a way to make money.

- Ask about aggression in the parents. Also find out if the breeders have other dog breeds in the home. While puppies are more temperamentally malleable than adults, if a Shar-Pei has had some exposure to other breeds, it may make it easier to integrate him into a home that already has dogs.

Contracts And Guarantees

Breeder contracts and guarantees are meant to protect the puppies as much as they are meant to protect you. If a breeder has a contract that must be signed, make sure that you read through it completely and are willing to meet all of the requirements prior to signing it. The contracts tend to be fairly easy to understand and comply with, but you should be aware of

Photo Courtesy
of Lorraine Coupe

all the facts before you agree to anything. Beyond putting down the money for the puppy, signing the contract says that you are serious about how you plan to take care of the puppy to the best of your abilities by meeting the minimum requirements set forth by the breeder. A contract may also say that the breeder will retain the puppy's original registration papers, although you can get a copy of the papers.

When a family does not live up to the agreement in the contract, the breeder is able to take the puppy from that family. These are the dogs that some breeders have available for adoption.

The guarantee states what health condition the breeder promises for their puppies. This typically includes details about the dog's health and recommendations on the next steps of the puppy's care once it leaves the breeder's facility. Guarantees may also provide schedules to ensure that the health care started by the breeder is continued by the new puppy parent. In the event that a major health concern is found, the puppy will need to be returned to the breeder. The contract will also explain what is not guaranteed. The guarantee tends to be very long (sometimes longer than the contract), and you should read it thoroughly before you sign it.

Shar-Pei contracts usually come with a requirement to have the dog spayed or neutered once it reaches maturity (typically six months). The contract may also contain naming requirements, health details, and a stipulation for what will happen if you can no longer take care of the animal (the dog usually goes back to the breeder). It could also include information on what will happen if you are negligent or abusive to your dog.

Health Tests And Certifications

With a breed with so many potential genetic issues, you need to find a breeder who takes good breeding practices very seriously. A good breeder keeps extensive records of each puppy and the parents. You will want to review each of the parents' complete history to understand what traits your puppy is likely to inherit. Pay attention to learning abilities, temperament, clinginess, and any personality trait you consider important. You can either request that documents be sent electronically to you or get them when you visit the breeder in person.

It could take a while to review the breeder's information about each parent, but it is always well worth the time you spend studying and planning. The more you know about the parents, the better prepared you will be for your puppy.

When looking for a Shar-Pei to adopt, there are several health concerns that you should ask breeders or rescue groups about.

The following are health tests all breeders should ensure their Shar-Pei undergo:

- Hip Evaluation
- Elbow Evaluation
- Patella Evaluation
- Thyroid Evaluation
- Ophthalmologist Evaluation

Breeders who take the time to join one of the many Shar-Pei organizations prove that they are serious about the health of their puppies. This organization requires that a standardized set of requirements be met, so membership denotes that the breeders who join are reliable and reputable.

Selecting A Puppy From A Breeder

Selecting your puppy should be done in person. However, you can start checking out your puppy after birth if the breeder is willing to share videos and pictures. Once you are allowed to see the puppies in person, consider the following:

- Assess the group of puppies as a whole. If most or all of the puppies are aggressive or fearful, this is an indication of a problem with the litter or (more likely) the breeder. Here are a few red flags if they are displayed by a majority of the puppies:
  - Tucked tails
  - Shrinking away from people
  - Whimpering when people get close
  - Constant attacking of your hands or feet (beyond pouncing)
- Notice how well each puppy plays with the others. This is a great indicator of how well your puppy will react to any pets you already have at home.
- Notice which puppies greet you first, and which ones hang back to observe.

- The puppies should not be fat or underweight. A swollen stomach is generally a sign of worms or other health problems.

- Puppies should have straight, sturdy legs. Splayed legs can be a sign that there is something wrong.

- Examine the puppy's ears for mites, which will cause a discharge. The inside of the ear should be pink, not red or inflamed.

- The eyes should be clear and bright.

- Check the puppy's mouth for pink, healthy-looking gums.

- Pet the puppy to check his coat for the following:

  - Ensure that the coat feels thick and full. If the breeder has allowed the fur to get matted or really dirty, it is an indication that they likely are not taking proper care of the animals.

  - Check for fleas and mites by running your hand from the head to the tail, then under the tail (fleas are more likely to hide under dogs' tails). Mites may look like dandruff.

- Check the puppy's rump for redness and sores and see if you can check the last bowel movement to ensure it is firm.

Pick the puppy that exhibits the personality traits that you want in your dog. If you want a forward, friendly, excitable dog, the first puppy to greet you may be the one you seek. If you want a dog that will think things through and let others get more attention, look for a puppy that sits back and observes you before approaching.

CHAPTER 4
Preparing Your Family

"While a Shar-pei does not require a lot of exercise or special accommodations, they are extremely family oriented and early bonding and social interaction is important. A family who desires a canine companion that will be an integral part of their life is desired. Shar-pei do not do well in situations where they are left alone for long periods of time."

Debbie Raynor
DC Shar-pei

Photo Courtesy
of Zoe Phillips

Training starts from the moment you get your Shar-Pei. Your family will need to be reminded of this several times before the puppy or dog arrives so that they will be prepared to keep their excitement in check.

Beyond that, you will have a good number of tasks that need to be done before your new dog arrives. You must determine who will be responsible for the different needs of the dog, as well as determining where your new dog will be for at least the first couple of weeks (even an adult dog will want to have a dedicated space in the beginning as you get to know each other). You will need to establish who is the primary person responsible for the dog's care, and make sure all of the members of your family keep this in mind.

Instructing Children

You want your pup to feel comfortable from the start, which means making sure your children are careful and gentle with the dog, whether you're planning on adopting a puppy or an adult. This is a breed that looks absolutely adorable, and some kids may try to treat the puppy like a toy or stuffed animal, which could be detrimental to your Shar-Pei. You will have to make sure your kids follow all of the rules from the beginning to ensure that your puppy feels safe, happy, and isn't accidentally injured. Shar-Pei already tend to be wary of kids, so you need to make sure your dog doesn't have a reason to be uncomfortable around your children.

Photo Courtesy of Eva Mccallum

Photo Courtesy
of Maria Clayton

Remind your kids of the following rules regularly, both before the puppy arrives and after. Older teens will probably be all right to help with the puppy, but younger teens and kids should not be left alone with the puppy for a few months. Remember that you will need to be very firm to make sure that the puppy is not hurt or frightened.

> **The following are the five golden rules that your children should follow from the very first interaction.**
>
> **1.**   Always be gentle and respectful.
>
> **2.**   Do not disturb the puppy during mealtime.
>
> **3.**   Chase is an outside game.
>
> **4.**   The Shar-Pei should always remain firmly on the ground. Never pick him up.
>
> **5.**   All of your valuables should be kept well out of the puppy's reach.

Since your kids are going to ask why, here are the explanations you can give them. You can simplify them for younger kids, or use them to start a dialogue with teens.

Always Be Gentle And Respectful

Little Shar-Pei puppies are very cute and cuddly, but they are also more fragile than adults. At no time should anyone play rough with the puppy (or any adult Shar-Pei). It is important to be respectful of your puppy to help the dog learn to also be respectful toward people and other animals.

This rule must be applied consistently every time your children play with the puppy. Be firm if you see your children getting too excited or rough. You don't want the puppy to get overly excited either because he might end up nipping or biting someone. If he does, it isn't his fault because he hasn't learned better yet – it is the child's fault. Make sure your children understand the possible repercussions if they get too rough.

Mealtime

Shar-Pei, like nearly every breed, can be protective of their food, especially if you rescue a dog that has previously had to fend for himself. Even if you have a puppy, you don't want him to feel insecure about his food because that will teach him to be aggressive when he is eating. Save yourself, your family, and your dog trouble by making sure everyone knows that eating time is your dog's time alone. Similarly, teach your kids that their own mealtime is off limits to the puppy. No feeding him from the table.

Chase

Make sure your kids understand why a game of chase is fine outside (though you'll need to monitor it), but inside the house the game is off limits.

Running inside the home gives your Shar-Pei puppy the impression that your home isn't safe inside because he is being chased. And it teaches your puppy that running indoors is fine, which can be very dangerous as the dog gets older and bigger. One of the last things you want is for your adult Shar-Pei to go barreling through your home knocking into people because it was fine for him to run in the house when he was a puppy.

Photo Courtesy
of Megan Whittaker

Paws On The Ground

No one should be picking the puppy up. Kids particularly have trouble understanding since they will see the Shar-Pei puppy as being more like a toy than a living creature. The younger your children are, the more difficult it will be for them to understand the difference.

It is so tempting to treat the puppy like a baby and to try to carry him around like one, but this is incredibly uncomfortable and unhealthy for the puppy. Older kids will quickly learn that a puppy's nip or bite hurts a lot more than you would think. Those little teeth are quite sharp, and you don't want the puppy to be dropped. If your children learn never to pick up the puppy, things will go a lot better. Remember, this also applies to you, so don't make things difficult by doing something you constantly tell your children not to do.

Keep Valuables Out Of Reach

Valuables are not something you want to end up in the puppy's mouth, whether it's toys, jewelry, or shoes. Your kids will be less than happy if their personal possessions are chewed up by an inquisitive puppy, so teach them to put toys, clothes, and other valuables far out of the puppy's reach.

Preparing Your Current Dogs

Shar-Pei tend to want to be in charge, so you are going to need to prepare your current pup for a new dog because life will change with the arrival of a Shar-Pei – and the hierarchy will likely shift was well. This means if you already have canines in your home, they need to be prepared for the new arrival.

Here are the important tasks to do to prepare your current pets for your new arrival.

- Set a schedule for activities and the people who will need to participate.
- Preserve your current dogs' favorite places and furniture, and make sure their toys and items are not in the puppy's space.
- Have playdates at your home and analyze your dogs to see how they react to an addition.

Photo Courtesy of Kylie McKinnon

Stick To A Schedule

Obviously, the puppy is going to get a lot of attention, so you need to make a concerted effort to let any current pets know that you still love and care for them. Make a specific time in your schedule just for your current dog or dogs, and make sure that you don't stray from that schedule after the puppy's arrival.

Make sure that you plan to have at least one adult around for each dog you have. Cats are a cause for concern, and you will probably want to have at least one other adult around (especially if you adopt an adult) when the puppy comes home. We will go into more detail later about what the roles of the other adults will be, but, for now, when you know what date you will be bringing your puppy home, ensure that you have additional adults to help out. You may need to remind them as the time nears, so set an alert on your phone, as well as the date, time, and pickup information for your puppy.

One benefit of having a schedule for your other dogs in place before your Shar-Pei puppy arrives is that it will then be easy to keep a schedule with the puppy. Shar-Pei love to know what to expect, at least in the beginning.

Your puppy is going to eat, sleep, and spend most of the day and night in his assigned space. This means that the space cannot block your current canine from his favorite furniture, bed, or any place where he rests over the course of the day. None of your current dog's stuff should be in this area, and this includes toys. You don't want your dog to feel like the puppy is taking over his territory. Make sure your children understand to never to put your current dog's stuff in the puppy's area.

Your dog and the puppy will need to be kept apart in the early days (even if they seem friendly), until your puppy is done with his vaccinations. Puppies are more susceptible to illness during these days, so wait until the puppy is protected before the dogs spend time together. Leaving the puppy in the puppy space will keep them separated during this critical time.

Helping Your Dog Prepare – Extra At Home Playdates

Here are things that will best help prepare your pooch for the arrival of your puppy.

- Think about your dog's personality to help you decide the best way to prepare for that first day, week, and month. Each dog is unique, so you will need to consider your dog's personality to determine how things will go when the new dog arrives. If your current dog loves other dogs, this will probably hold true when the puppy shows up. If your dog has any territorial tendencies, you will need to be cautious about the introduction and first couple of months so that your current dog learns that the Shar-Pei is now a part of the pack. Excitable dogs will need special attention to keep them from getting overly agitated when a new dog comes home. You don't want them to be so excited they make the Shar-Pei feel threatened.

- Consider the times when you have had other dogs in your home and how your current dog reacted to these other furry visitors. If your canine displayed territorial tendencies, you should be extra careful with how you introduce your new pup. If you haven't ever invited another dog to your home, have a couple of playdates with other dogs at your home before your new Shar-Pei puppy arrives. You have to know how your current furry babies will react to new dogs in the house so you can properly prepare. Meeting a dog at home is very different from encountering one outside the home.

- Think about your dog's interactions with other dogs for as long as you have known the pup. Has your dog shown either protective or possessive behavior, either with you or others? Some dogs can be protective of food, people and/or toys.

- If you know someone with a Shar-Pei, it would be great to have playdates with that dog so that your current dog is already aware of the temperament of the breed. If not, any other breed known for being guard dogs can help, such as a German Shephard, Akita, Cane Corso, Doberman Pinscher, or Rottweiler. Every dog may be different, but the guardian breeds have very similar tendencies, including a wariness of others. This may help your dog learn how to be more measured in the approach to a Shar-Pei. Of course, if you are bringing a puppy home, this will not be as much of a concern, but it could still be helpful.

The same rules apply, no matter how many dogs you have. Think about the personalities of all of them as individuals, as well as how they interact together. Just like people, you may find that when they are together your dogs act differently, which you will need to keep in mind as you plan their first introduction.

See Chapter 8 for planning to introduce your current dogs and your new puppy, and how to juggle a new puppy and your current pets.

Not A Fan Of Other Dogs, May Not Care For Other Pets

Shar-Pei were a favorite fighting dog for centuries, so they are generally wary and aggressive toward other pets. They don't tend to like cats very much either. They were herders for millennia, so they have a tendency to chase and corral smaller animals. Shar-Pei were also hunters, so they may not see the cats as being other pets.

As soon as your puppy is fully vaccinated, you will need to start teaching him to socialize. Once that happens, your Shar-Pei will see the other pets as a part of the family. This likely will not transfer to other animals outside the home, but he will be protective of your other pets instead of aggressive towards them.

FUN FACT
Unique Tongue

The Shar-Pei is one of only two dog breeds to have a blue-black tongue. The other is another Chinese dog breed, the Chow Chow. It's thought that the dark tongue was to help the dog look more ferocious or ward off evil spirits. Interestingly, Shar Pei with lighter coat types tend to have lavender tongues.

CHAPTER 5
Preparing Your Home And Schedule

"Shar-Pei are very family oriented. They are loyal and prefer to be with their humans whether it is sitting on the couch, out for a walk, or car ride, or even doing agility."

Janet Saporito
Thornapple Hill Chinese Shar-Pei

Even if you select an adult dog, there is going to be a lot of preparation because the house is secure for both the dog's security and your own. You have to remember that Shar-Pei are smart dogs, and they can figure things out that you would not expect. That unique, wise appearance should be a good reminder that your adult Shar-Pei has a real brain inside that sizeable head. That means that he will be looking around, seeing just what he can explore.

The week before your puppy arrives, you should conduct numerous checks to ensure that your home is safe for the new family member. Making sure your new Shar-Pei has a safe space with all of the essentials (including toys) will make the arrival of your newest family addition a great time for everyone – especially your new canine companion.

Even if you bring an adult Shar-Pei home, you have to prepare for the arrival of an incredibly headstrong toddler that will need convincing that there is a good reason to listen to you. Shar-Pei have to learn that you are in control, which means that you have to gain their respect before they will listen to you, and, even after that, they may not want to listen to you all of the time. If your dog has not already learned not to grab food, climb on furniture, or whatever other restrictions you have implemented in your home, you will have your work cut out for you when it comes to training your new friend. Dog-proofing your home will help you keep your dog safe while he is learning to listen to you.

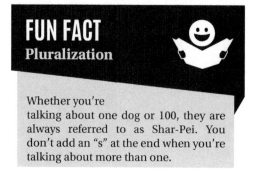

FUN FACT
Pluralization

Whether you're talking about one dog or 100, they are always referred to as Shar-Pei. You don't add an "s" at the end when you're talking about more than one.

Photo Courtesy of Megan Yiu

Planning The First Year's Budget

Caring for a puppy is a lot more expensive than you would think. You will want to have a budget, which is a good reason to start purchasing supplies a few months in advance. When you buy the items you need, you will begin to see exactly how much you will spend a month. Of course there are some items that are one-time purchases, but many other items will have to be purchased regularly, like food and treats.

Begin budgeting the day you decide to get your puppy. The cost will include the adoption fee, which is typically higher for a purebred dog than for a rescue dog.

The vet and other healthcare costs, such as regular vaccinations and an annual checkup, should be included in your budget.

The following table can help you start to plan your budget. Keep in mind that the prices are rough averages, and may be significantly different based on where you live.

Item	Considerations	Estimated Costs
Crate	You will need two crates: one for the puppy and one for when the puppy grows up. This should be a comfortable space where the puppy will sleep and rest.	Wire crates: Range $60 to $350 Portable crate: Range $35 to $200
Bed	You will probably need two beds: one for the puppy, and one for when the pup grows up. This will be placed in the crate.	$10 to $55
Leash	It should be short in the beginning because you need to be able to keep your puppy from getting overexcited and running to the end of a long line.	Short leash: $6 to $15
Doggie bags for walks	For those who don't have daily access to bags, it is best to purchase packs to ensure you don't run out.	Singles cost less than $1 each. Packs: $4 to $16
Collar	You will likely need two collars: one for a puppy, and one for an adult Shar-Pei.	$10 to $30
Tags	These will likely be provided by your vet. Find out what information the vet provides for tags, then purchase any tags that are not provided. At a minimum, your Shar-Pei should have tags with your address on it in case the pup escapes.	Contact your vet before purchasing to see if the required rabies tags include your contact info.
Puppy food	This depends on if you plan to make your Shar-Pei food, prefer to purchase food, or both. The larger the bag, the higher the cost, but the fewer times you will need to purchase food. You will need to purchase puppy-specific food the first year. Adult dog food is more expensive, particularly for large breeds like the Shar-Pei.	$9 to $90 per bag

Water and food bowls	These will need to be kept in the puppy's area. If you have other dogs, you will need separate bowls for the puppy.	$10 to $40
Toothbrush/ Toothpaste	You will need to brush your dog's teeth regularly, so plan to use more than one toothbrush during the first year.	$2.50 t0 $14
Brush	Shar-Pei coats are incredibly easy to maintain, but you should still brush them regularly. When they are puppies, brushing offers a great way to bond.	$3.50 to $20
Toys	If you want to postpone purchasing toys, that is fine. Shar-Pei don't tend to like toys. If you have a puppy, you may be able to teach the little guy to play, but there are cheaper alternatives with Shar-Pei than toys.	$2.00 Packs of toys range from $10 to $20 (easier in the long run as your pup will chew through toys quickly)
Training treats	You will need these from the beginning, and likely won't need to change the treats based on your Shar-Pei's age; you may need to change treats to keep your dog's interest though.	$4.50 to $15

You won't need to purchase the adult version of these items before the puppy arrives, but you will need to have them within the first 6 months because your puppy is going to grow fast. Set up a budget for the initial costs, then a second budget for adult versions of items that will need to be replaced as the puppy grows.

To help you create your list for a new puppy, you will just the need following supplies. The list is longer than most people realize, so take some time to really think about what you will need based on your home and circumstances. If you start making purchases around the time you identify the breeder you will get the puppy from, you can stretch out your expenses over a longer period of time. This will make it seem a lot less expensive than it actually is. The following are recommended items you should have purchased before bringing your new dog home:

- Crate
- Bed
- Leash
- Doggie bags for walks
- Collar
- Tags
- Puppy food/adult food (depending on age of dog)

- Water and food bowls (sharing a water bowl is usually okay, but your puppy needs his or her own food dish if you have multiple dogs)
- Toothbrush/Toothpaste
- Brush
- Toys
- Training treats

Photo Courtesy of Kathryn Bateman

Talk to your vet before buying any medications, including flea treatments. The rest of the supplies from the annual budget can be postponed until a later date when you need them. Some of them you probably won't need for a couple of years when your pup becomes an adult.

Creating A Safe Space For Your Dog Or Puppy

Your puppy will need a dedicated space that includes a crate (more information on this in the next section), food and water bowls, pee pads, and toys. All of these things will need to be in the area where the puppy will be when you are not able to give him attention. The puppy space should be gated so that the puppy cannot get out, and young children and other dogs cannot get in. It should be a safe space where the puppy can see you going about your usual business and feel comfortable.

Crates And Crate Training

Crate training a Shar-Pei puppy can be fairly easy, but not if you have a crate that is too big, too small, or too hard for your dog to feel like it is a safe place. To make training easy later, you need to ensure that the puppy's crate and bedding are already set up and ready before your puppy arrives.

Never treat the crate like it is a prison for your puppy. It's meant to be a safe haven after overstimulation or when it's time to sleep. Ensure your dog never associates the crate with punishment or negative emotions. The crate should be adjustable so that you can make it a bit larger when your puppy becomes an adult. You can also get your puppy a carrying crate in the early days to make trips to the vet a little easier. This crate won't work when your Shar-Pei is an adult (you can just walk your dog into the vet's office as an adult), but a carrying crate has plenty of space for a puppy.

As mentioned in an earlier chapter, you can use the crate to help with housetraining. The Shar-Pei is one of the easier breeds to housetrain, which is probably a welcome piece of news. You may want to have a pee pad in the puppy's area as far from the crate as possible because your Shar-Pei will likely want to keep the immediate area around his bed clean. This will also give your puppy a place to go during inclement weather. Make sure to find out from the breeder if the puppy has already begun housetraining. If the puppy is already making progress, you may not want to add the pee pad since that can be confusing to the puppy.

Puppy-Proof The House

Preparing for the arrival of a puppy is time consuming, and all of the most dangerous rooms and items in your home will be equally as dangerous to your puppy as they would be to a baby. The biggest difference is that your Shar-Pei is going to be mobile much faster than a child. He will potentially get into dangerous situations almost immediately if you don't eliminate all of the dangers ahead of his arrival in your home.

Be aware that puppies will try to eat virtually anything. Nothing is safe – not even your furniture. They'll gnaw on wood and metal. Anything within their reach is considered to be fair game. Keep this in mind as you go about puppy-proofing your home.

Indoor Hazards And Fixes

Photo Courtesy of Randy Celaya

This section details the areas inside your home where you should focus your attention. In case of problems, have your vet's number posted on the fridge and in at least one other room in the house. If you set this up before your pup arrives, it will be there if you need it. Even if you program the vet's phone number into your phone, another family member or someone taking care of your Shar-Pei may still need it so have the vet's number conveniently posted.

Shar-Pei will almost certainly be an avid explorer, wanting to get into everything if given the opportunity. Get low and see each room from your Shar-Pei's perspective; you are almost guaranteed to find at least one thing you missed when you do your final check.

Hazards	Fixes	Time Estimate
Kitchen		
Poisons	Keep in secured, childproof cabinets or on high shelves	30 min
Trash cans	Have a lockable trash can, or keep it in a secured location	10 min
Appliances	Make sure all cords are out of reach	15 min
Human Food	Keep out of reach	Constant (start making it a habit)
Floors		
Slippery surfaces	Put down rugs or special mats designed to stick to the floor	30 min – 1 hour
Training area	Train on non-slip surfaces	Constant
Bathrooms		
Toilet brush	Either have one that locks or keep out of reach	5 min/bathroom
Poisons	Keep in secured, childproof cabinets or on high shelves	15 – 30 min/ bathroom
Toilets	Keep lids closed Do not use automatic toilet cleaning chemicals	Constant (start making it a habit)
Cabinets	Keep locked with child-proof locks	15 – 30 min/ bathroom
Laundry Room		
Clothing	Store clean and dirty clothing off the floor, and out of reach	15 – 30 min
Poisons (bleach, pods/detergent, dryer sheets, and misc. poisons)	Keep in secured, child-proofed cabinets or on high shelves	15 min
Around the Home		
Plants	Keep off the floor	45 min – 1 hour
Trash cans	Have a lockable trash can, or keep it in a secured location	30 min

Electrical cords, window blind cords	Hide them or make sure they are out of reach; pay particular attention to entertainment and computer areas	1.5 hours
Poisons	Check to make sure there aren't any in reach (WD40, window/screen cleaner, carpet cleaner, air fresheners); move all poisons to a centralized, locked location	1 hour
Windows	Check that cords are out of reach in all rooms	1 – 2 hours
Fireplaces	Store cleaning supplies and tools where the puppy can't get into them Cover the fireplace opening with something the puppy can't knock over	10 min/fireplace
Stairs	Cordon off so that your puppy can't try to go up or down them; make sure to test any puppy gates	10 – 15 min
Coffee tables/End tables/Nightstands	Clear of dangerous objects (e.g., scissors, sewing equipment, pens, and pencils) and all valuables	30 – 45 min

If you have a cat, keep the litter box up off the floor. It needs to be somewhere that your cat can easily get to but your Shar-Pei cannot. Since this involves teaching your cat to use the new area, it's something you should do well in advance of the puppy's arrival. You don't want your cat to undergo too many significant changes all at once. The puppy will be enough of a disruption; if your cat associates the change with the puppy, you may find the feline protesting by refusing to use the litter box.

Outdoor Hazards And Fixes

This section details the things outside your home that need your attention ahead of your puppy's arrival. Also post the vet's number in one of the sheltered areas in case of an emergency.

*Photo Courtesy
of Marie Collins*

Hazards	Fixes	Time Estimate
Garage		
Poisons	Keep in secured, child-proofed cabinets or on high shelves (e.g., car chemicals, cleaning supplies, paint, lawn care) – this includes fertilizer	1 hour
Trash bins	Keep them in a secured location	5 min
Tools (e.g., lawn, car, hardware, power tools)	Make sure all cords are kept out of reach and never hanging over the side of surfaces	30 min – 1 hour
Equipment (e.g., sports, fishing)	Keep out of reach and never hanging over the side of surfaces	Constant (start making it a habit)
Sharp implements	Keep out of reach and never hanging over the side of surfaces	30 min
Bikes	Store off the ground or in a place the Shar-Pei cannot get to (to keep the pup from biting the tires)	20 min
Fencing (Can Be Done Concurrently)		
Breaks	Fix any breaks in the fencing. You need to make sure your Shar-Pei can't easily get out of your yard.	30 min – 1 hour
Gaps	Fill any gaps, even if they are intentional, so your Shar-Pei doesn't escape	30 min – 1 hour
Holes/Dips at Base	Fill any area that can be easily crawled under	1 – 2 hours

Yard		
Poisons	Don't leave any poisons in the yard	1 – 2 hours
Plants	Verify that all low plants aren't poisonous to dogs; fence off anything that is (such as grape vines)	45 min – 1 hour
Tools (e.g., lawn maintenance and gardening tools)	Make sure they are out of reach; Make sure nothing is hanging over the sides of outdoor tables	30 min – 1 hour

Never leave your Shar-Pei alone in the garage, even when he is an adult. It is likely that your puppy will be in the garage when you take car trips, which is why it is important to puppy-proof it.

Shar-Pei aren't notorious diggers, but that doesn't mean they won't do it when they get bored. Leaving them in the yard is a good way to end up with holes where your flowers used to be. Odds are, your dog will try to bury something he loves for a later time. There's no reason to get mad at your

Photo Courtesy
of Chanelle Ross

Photo Courtesy
of Arik Mukai

dog because that simply does not work on the Shar-Pei, especially since he won't understand there being anything wrong with digging. Since it isn't likely that digging will be a significant problem, you can avoid it by simply being outside with your Shar-Pei. You can also create a specific space for digging then encourage the behavior in that particular area.

Fence inspections are an activity you are going to need to continue to schedule at least once a month.

Just like with the inside, you will need to follow up your outdoor preparations by getting down low and checking out all areas from a puppy's perspective. Again, you are all but guaranteed to find at least one thing you missed.

Choosing Your Veterinarian

Start looking around for a vet for your Shar-Pei even before you choose a breeder. You should have your vet chosen before you bring your dog home. Whether you get a puppy or an adult, you should take your canine to the vet within 48 hours (24 hours is strongly recommended) of his arrival to make sure your dog is healthy. If there is a vet near you who specializes in or has worked with Shar-Pei before, that will be best for your pup. Considering the Shar-Pei's personality, you want a vet who knows how to work with a headstrong pooch. Getting an appointment with a vet can take a while, especially one that specializes in a particular breed, just like getting a doctor's appointment. You need to have your vet and the first appointment booked well in advance of your dog's arrival.

Here are some things to consider when looking for a vet:

● **What is the vet's level of familiarity with Shar-Pei?**

The vet doesn't have to be a specialist, but if you can find a vet with some experience with the canine breed, the vet can help you know what to expect in the different stages of your dog's life. Considering that Shar-Pei aren't very common, you may not be able to find a vet with experience. If that is the case, find out if the vet has experience with other guardian breeds (such as Rottweilers and German Shepherds, two more common breeds) and mastiffs. Experience with these breeds isn't quite the same as experience with Shar-Pei, but it will give the vet some idea of what to look for in your dog.

● **How far from your home is the vet?**

You don't want the vet to be more than 30 minutes away in case of an emergency.

Photo Courtesy
of Kimberly Georgeff

- Is the vet available for emergencies after hours or can they recommend a vet in case of an emergency?

- Is the vet part of a local vet hospital if needed, or does the doctor refer patients to a local pet hospital?

- Is the vet the only vet or one of several partners? If he or she is part of a partnership, can you stick with just one vet for office visits?

- How are appointments booked?

- Can you have other services performed there, such as grooming and boarding?

- Is the vet accredited?

- What are the prices for the initial visit and the normal costs, such as for shots and regular visits?

- What tests and checks are performed during the initial visit?

Before bringing your dog home, make time to visit the vet you are considering so that you can look around to see what the environment is like inside the office. Ask if you can speak to the vet to see if he or she is willing to help put you at ease and answer your questions. A vet's time is valuable, but he or she should have a few minutes to help you feel confident that he/she is the right choice to help take care of your canine.

CHAPTER 6
Bringing Your Shar-Pei Home

"Remember that your puppy has just been taken away from his first born family. This is a time of transition. Offer love and support while being aware that he may cry or whine during the first few days. Having the breeder rub a small blanket or toy on the littermates and mom to get their scent can help with this initial transition. It will also help to try and keep your puppy on the same schedule he was on at the breeders home, at least for a few weeks. Any changes in schedule or diet need to be done gradually."

Debbie Raynor
DC Shar-pei

Photo Courtesy
of Cielo Phillips

Few things in your life will be as memorable and exciting as bringing your Shar-Pei home. It's fun and exciting as you watch your new family member try to figure out that this is his new home. But keep in mind that while you are getting to know your new dog, your new dog is having get to know both the family and a new home. It can be overwhelming, regardless of the dog's age. You never know exactly how your puppy or adult dog will react, but you know there is going to be just as much uncertainty on his part as there is on yours.

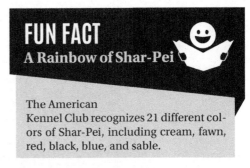

FUN FACT
A Rainbow of Shar-Pei

The American Kennel Club recognizes 21 different colors of Shar-Pei, including cream, fawn, red, black, blue, and sable.

Make sure to read Chapter 7 about how to introduce your adult dog to a multi-pet home. Shar-Pei can be aggressive with other dogs, so you need to make sure that everyone feels comfortable. Regardless of if you bring home a puppy or an adult, you will need a special, prepared space where your other dogs can't go, and preferably where your cat can't go either. You want to make sure to take it slow in the early days to introduce and socialize your new dog.

Final Preparations And Planning

Most intelligent breeds require a constant presence for the first week and as much of the first month as possible. They can figure out a way of escaping from their enclosure, so you need someone home to stop any escape attempts. You should plan to take time off from work or negotiate working from home during at least the first 24 hours, if not the first 48 hours. The best-case scenario would have you being at home for the first week or two. The more time you can dedicate to helping your new little friend become accustomed to his new surroundings in those first few days, the better for your new family member and the more quickly your pup will feel comfortable in his new environment.

The following are some useful checklists to get you through the preparation for your puppy and the aftermath of his arrival at your home.

Ensure You Have Food And Other Supplies On Hand

Do a quick check to ensure that you have everything you need. If you created a list based on the basic supplies from Chapter 5, review the list the day before your Shar-Pei arrives and make sure you have everything on it.

Photo Courtesy of Christopher Roes

Take a few moments to consider if there is anything you are missing, too. This will hopefully save you from having to try to rush out to buy additional supplies after the arrival of your new family member.

Design A Tentative Puppy Schedule

Prepare a tentative schedule to help you get started over the course of the first week. Your days are about to get very busy, so you need somewhere to start before your puppy arrives. The following are the three important areas to have established for your puppy's schedule:

- Feeding

- Training (including housetraining)

- Playing

When you bring home a puppy, you may be expecting high energy. However, puppies of any breed (no matter how active they will be later) require a lot of sleep. Expect your puppy to sleep between 18 and 20 hours per day. Having a predictable sleep schedule will help your puppy to grow up healthier.

In the beginning, you won't need to worry about making sure that your puppy is tired out by the end of the day. His stamina will build fairly quickly, though, so by the end of the first year your pup will be a lot more active. One of the best things about the breed is that they tend to have energy levels appropriate to their situation, so you aren't going to be as hard pressed to tire your Shar-Pei out as you would a Beagle or Jack Russell Terrier. You will still need to make sure that he gets enough exercise based on his caloric intake, especially if you tend to be more sedentary. Shar-Pei will adapt to your exercise habits, but they do still need regular exercise.

In the early days, your puppy's schedule will largely revolve around sleeping and eating, with some walking and socialization. Waking hours will include training and play.

Do A Quick Final Puppy-Proofing Inspection Before The Puppy Arrives

No matter how busy you are, or how carefully you followed the puppy-proofing checklists from the previous chapter, you still need to take the time to inspect your home one more time before the puppy arrives. Set aside an hour or two to complete this a day or two before the puppy arrives.

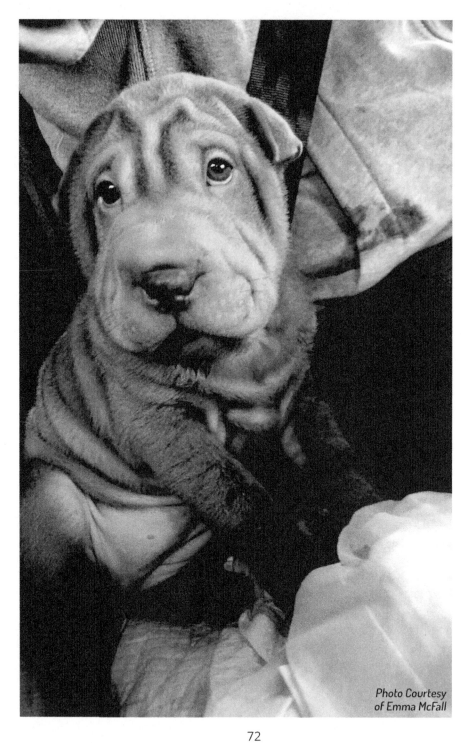

*Photo Courtesy
of Emma McFall*

Initial Meeting

Have a meeting with all of the family members to make sure all of the rules discussed in Chapter 4 are remembered and understood before the puppy is a distraction. This includes how to handle the puppy. Determine who is going to be responsible for primary puppy care, including who will be the primary trainer. To help teach younger children about responsibility, a parent can pair with a child to manage the puppy's care. The child can be responsible for things like keeping the water bowl filled and feeding the puppy, while a parent oversees the tasks.

Picking Up Your Puppy Or Dog And The Ride Home

Picking up your puppy takes a good bit of planning and preparation, especially if you are going to the breeder's home. If possible, plan to pick up your puppy on a weekend or at the beginning of a holiday so you can spend unrushed time at home with him. This section covers the preparation and actual trip, but not what to do if you have other dogs that you need to introduce (Chapter 8).

As tempting as it is to cuddle with your puppy, using a crate for the ride home is both safer and more comfortable for the puppy. Two adults should be present on the first trip.

- The crate should be anchored in the car for safety and include a cushion. If you have a long trip, bring food and water and plan to stop to give them to the puppy during intervals of the trip. Do not put these in the crate as they will not be anchored down, and sloshing water can scare your puppy. You can cover the bottom of the crate with a towel or pee pad in case of accidents.

- Call the breeder to make sure everything is still on schedule and make sure the puppy is ready.

- Ask, if you haven't already, if you can get the mother to leave her scent on a blanket to help make the puppy's transition more comfortable.

- Make sure the other adult remembers and will be on time to head to the pick-up destination.

- If you have other dogs, make sure that all of the adults involved know what to do, the time and where to go for that first neutral territory meeting.

If you do not have other dogs, you can pick up your puppy and head straight home. If you have a long trip (more than a couple of hours), build breaks into it every few hours to give your puppy a chance to stretch, exercise, drink, and use the bathroom. Do not leave the puppy alone in the car for any amount of time. If you have to use the restroom, at least one adult must remain with the puppy during each stop.

Ask the breeder if the puppy has been in a car before, and, if not, it is especially important to have someone who can give the puppy attention while the other person drives. The puppy will be in the crate, but someone can still provide comfort. It will definitely be scary because the puppy no longer has mom, siblings, or known people around, so having someone present to talk to the puppy will make it less of an ordeal for the little guy.

This is the time to start teaching your puppy that car trips are enjoyable. This means making sure that the crate is securely anchored. You don't want to terrify the puppy by letting the crate slide around while he is sitting helpless inside it.

When you arrive home, immediately take the puppy or dog outside to use the bathroom. Even if the puppy or dog had an accident on the way, this is the time to start training your new family member where to use the bathroom.

The First Vet Visit And What To Expect

A vet's visit is necessary within the first day or two of your puppy's arrival and may be required in the contract you signed with the breeder. You need to establish a baseline for the puppy's health so that the vet can track your puppy's progress and monitor to ensure everything is going well as your Shar-Pei grows. The initial assessment gives you more information about your puppy, as well as giving you a chance to ask the vet questions and get advice. It also creates an important rapport between your Shar-Pei and the vet.

That first vet visit will be interesting and very different from subsequent visits. Your pup won't know what to expect since he hasn't been to that particular vet before. Try as best as you can to ease his anxiety. You want this first visit to set a positive tone for all future visits.

There are several things that you will need to do before the day of the appointment:

- Find out how early you need to arrive to complete the paperwork for the new patient.
- Find out if you should bring a stool sample for that first visit, too. If so, collect it the morning of the visit and make sure to take it with you.
- Bring in the paperwork provided by the breeder or rescue organization for the vet to add to your pup's or dog's records.

Upon your arrival, your puppy may want to meet the other pups and people in the office, which is something that can be encouraged as long as you keep some basic rules in mind. After all, this is a chance for you to work on socializing the puppy and to create an initial positive experience to associate with the vet, although you will need to be careful. Always ask the owner if it is all right for your puppy to meet their pet, and wait for approval before letting your puppy move forward with meeting other animals. Pets at the vet's office are very likely to not be feeling great, which means they may not be very affable. You don't want a grumpy older dog or a sick animal to nip or scare your puppy. Negative social experiences are something your puppy will remember, and will make going to the vet something to dread or resist. Nor do you want your puppy to be exposed to potential illnesses while he is still getting his shots.

During the first visit, the vet will conduct an initial assessment of your Shar-Pei. One of the most important things the vet will do is take your puppy's weight. This is something you are going to have to monitor for your Shar-Pei's entire life because the breed is prone to obesity. Record the weight for yourself so you can see how quickly the puppy is growing. Ask your vet what a healthy weight is at each stage, and record that as well. Shar-Pei grow unbelievably fast during the first year, but you should still make sure your dog isn't gaining more weight than is healthy.

The vet will set the date for the next set of shots, which will likely happen not too long after your puppy arrives. When it is time for his vaccinations, be prepared for a day or two of your puppy feeling under the weather.

Crate And Other Preliminary Training

"If you begin to crate train, don't be surprised when they howl and cry. It is a battle of wills that you must win. If you allow your Pei to come into your room and sleep in your bed, then you have lost the battle and they will be there forever."

Kathleen Probst
Conrad Knoll Chinese Shar-Pei

As mentioned, training starts from the moment your Shar-Pei becomes your responsibility. Considering the fact that your dog may be stubborn, you want to start getting your pup used to the idea that you are in charge. This will help play against the Shar-Pei's headstrong nature. Don't expect training to eliminate the behavior, but you can at least let your new pup know what the hierarchy is.

Photo Courtesy of Blair Mason

Puppies younger than six months old shouldn't be in the crate for hours at a time. They will not be able to hold their bladders that long, so you need to make sure they have a way to get out and use the restroom in an acceptable place. If you get an adult dog that is not housetrained, you will need to follow the same rules.

Make sure the door is set so that it doesn't close on your dog during his initial sniff of the crate. You don't want your Shar-Pei to get hit by the door as it is closing and have it scare him.

Repeat this for several weeks until your dog feels comfortable in the crate. Doing this several times each day can help your dog to learn that everything is all right and that the crate is not a punishment. Initially, you will be doing this while you are still at home or when you go out to get the

STEPS TO INTRODUCING YOUR PUPPY TO THEIR CRATE

1 **LET YOUR SHAR-PEI SNIFF THE CRATE.**
Talk to him while he does this, using a positive, happy voice. Associate the first experience in the crate with excitement and positive emotions so that your dog understands it is a good place. If you have a blanket from the puppy's mother, put it in the crate to help provide an extra sense of comfort.

2 **DROP A COUPLE OF TREATS INTO THE CRATE**
if your canine seems reluctant to enter it. Do NOT force your dog into the crate. If your dog doesn't want to go all the way into this strange little space, that is perfectly fine. It has to be his decision to enter so that it isn't a negative experience.

3 **FEED YOUR DOG IN THE CRATE FOR A WEEK OR TWO.**
This will help create some positive emotions with the crate, as well as helping you to keep the food away from other pets if you have them.
a. If your dog appears comfortable with the crate, put the food all the way at the back of the crate.
b. If not, place the food bowl in the front, then move it further back in the crate over time.

4 **START CLOSING THE DOOR**
once your dog appears to be eating comfortably in the crate. When the food is gone, open the crate immediately.

5 **LEAVE THE DOOR CLOSED**
for longer periods of time after your dog has eaten. If your pup begins to whine, you have left your Shar-Pei in the crate for too long.

6 **CRATE YOUR DOG FOR LONGER PERIODS OF TIME**
once your dog shows no signs of discomfort in the crate when he is eating. You can start to train him to go into the crate by simply saying "crate" or "bed," then praise your dog to let him know that he has done a great job.

mail. As soon as your puppy can make it for half an hour without whining while you're out of the room, you can start leaving your pup alone while you are gone, keeping the time to no more than an hour in the beginning.

The focus during these first few weeks is to start housetraining and minimize any undesirable behavior. Training from the start is vital, but don't take your new puppy to any classes just yet. This is because most puppies have not had all of the necessary shots, and good trainers will not allow them in classes until the full first round of shots is complete. Chapters 10 and 12 provide a closer look at the different kinds of training you should begin and how to follow through after the first few weeks.

First Night Frights

That first night is going to be scary to your little Shar-Pei puppy. As understandable as this may be, there is only so much comfort you can give your new family member. Just like with a baby, the more you respond to cries and whimpering, the more you are teaching a puppy that negative behaviors will provide the desired results. You will need to be prepared for a balancing act to provide reassurance that things will be all right while keeping your puppy from learning that crying gets your attention.

Create a sleeping area just for your puppy near where you sleep. The area should have the puppy's bed tucked safely into a crate. It offers him a safe place to hide so that he can feel more comfortable in a strange new home. The entire area should be blocked off so that no one can get into it (and the puppy can't get out) during the night. It should also be close to where people sleep so that the puppy doesn't feel abandoned. If you were able to get a blanket or pillow that smells like the mother, make sure this is in your puppy's space. Consider adding a little white noise to cover unfamiliar sounds that could scare your new pet.

Your puppy will make noises over the course of the night. Don't move the puppy away, even if the whimpering keeps you awake. If you give in, over time the whimpering, whining, and crying will get louder. Being moved away from people will only scare the puppy more, reinforcing the anxiety he feels. During the night, your puppy is not whimpering because he's been in the crate too long; he's scared or wants someone to be with him – he's probably never been alone at night before arriving at your home. Spare yourself some trouble later by teaching the puppy that whimpering doesn't always work to get him out of the crate. Over time, simply being close to you at night will be enough to reassure your puppy that everything will be all right.

Puppies will need to go to the bathroom every two to three hours, and you will need to get up during the night to make sure your puppy understands that he is to always go to the bathroom either outside or on the pee pad. If you let it go at night, you are going to have a difficult time training him that he cannot go in the house later.

If you choose to let your dog on the bed, wait until he is fully house-trained. Otherwise you will need to replace your bed within a short time. It is best to simply keep your Shar-Pei off the furniture so that your pup doesn't get hurt and your furniture is not ruined.

CHAPTER 7
The Multi-Pet Household

Bringing a Shar-Pei into a home with other pets can be challenging, especially if the dog is an adult. Shar-Pei don't tend to like other dogs unless they are properly socialized when they are young. There are a number of benefits to already having a dog in your home. If you bring home an adult that has been socialized, your current dog can help teach your new Shar-Pei the rules (the Shar-Pei may or may not listen, but he will pick up on the behaviors and is more likely to imitate your other dog as long as it is clear the directions come from you). If you bring home a puppy, your current dog could be a great mentor to your puppy (depending on your dog's patience with puppies). Having another dog also makes socialization fairly easy because it's likely that your Shar-Pei will pick up on your other dog listening to you, which could make it easier to get the Shar-Pei to listen. This works both ways though. If your current dog or dogs have any undesirable behaviors, you may want to try to work those out before your puppy arrives, too – you don't want your Shar-Pei learning bad habits.

Photo Courtesy of Victoria Gajeski

Photo Courtesy
of Cortney Petrillo

Introducing Your New Puppy To Your Other Pets

"If you have a dog at home when you purchase your puppy, bring them both outside on neutral ground for an introduction. He is coming into another dog's territory. Take slow steps and keep a watchful eye on them for awhile. Most older dogs will accept a new puppy but there is always the exception."

Kathleen Probst
Conrad Knoll Chinese Shar-Pei

Always introduce all new dogs to your current dog or dogs, regardless of age, in a neutral place away from your home. Even if you have never had problems with your current dog, you are about to change his world. Select a park or other public area where your dog will not feel territorial and plan to introduce your dog to the puppy there. This gives the animals the opportunity to meet and get to know each other before entering your home together.

When introducing your dog and puppy, make sure you have at least one other adult with you so there's a person to manage each canine. If you

Photo Courtesy
of Jazzy Sithisack

have more than one dog, then you should have one adult per dog. This will make it easier to keep all of the dogs under control. Even the best dogs can get overly excited about meeting a puppy. One of the people who needs to be there is the person who is in charge of the pets in your home (or people if you have more than one person in charge). This helps establish the pack hierarchy.

Don't hold your puppy when the dogs meet. While you may want to protect the puppy and make him feel comfortable by holding him, it has the opposite effect. Your puppy will likely feel trapped, with no way to escape. Being on the ground means that the puppy can run if he feels the need to. Stand near the puppy with your feet a little bit apart. That way, if the puppy decides he needs to escape he can quickly hide behind your legs.

The puppy and each dog should have a few minutes to sniff each other, making sure that there is always some slack in the leash. This helps dogs feel more relaxed since they won't feel like you are trying to restrain them. Your dog will probably either want to play or will simply ignore the puppy.

- If the dogs want to play, just be careful that the dog doesn't accidentally hurt the puppy.

- If the dog ends up ignoring the puppy after an initial sniff, that is fine too.

If your dog's hackles are up or if he is clearly unhappy, keep the two apart until your dog seems more comfortable with the situation. Don't force the meeting.

The introduction could take a while, depending on each individual dog's personality. The friendlier and more accepting your dog is, the easier it will be to incorporate your new puppy into the home. For some dogs a week is enough time to start feeling comfortable together. For other dogs, it could take a couple of months before they are fully accepting of a new puppy. Since this is a completely new dynamic in your household, your current dog may not be pleased with you bringing a little bundle of energy into his daily life. This is enough to make anyone unhappy, but especially a dog that has grown accustomed to a certain lifestyle. The older your dog is, the more likely it is that a puppy will be an unwelcome addition. Older dogs can get cranky around a puppy that doesn't understand the rules or doesn't know when enough is enough. The goal is to make your puppy feel welcome and safe, while letting your older dog know that your love for him is just as strong as ever.

Once your new family member and the rest of the canine pack start to get acquainted and feel comfortable with each other, you can head home. As the dogs enter the house, they will have a bit more familiarity with each other, making your current dogs feel more comfortable with the new addition to the family.

Once you are home, take the dogs into the yard and remove the leashes. You will need one adult per dog, including the puppy. If they seem to be all right or the dog is indifferent to the puppy, you can let your dog inside, re-leash the puppy, and keep the puppy on the leash as you go inside (after showing him where he is supposed to do his business).

Put the puppy in the puppy area when the introductions are done. Make sure your dogs cannot get into this area, and that your puppy cannot get out.

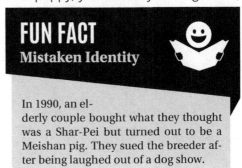

FUN FACT
Mistaken Identity

In 1990, an elderly couple bought what they thought was a Shar-Pei but turned out to be a Meishan pig. They sued the breeder after being laughed out of a dog show.

*Photo Courtesy
of Robin Schaufler*

Introducing An Adult Dog To Other Animals

You always need to approach the introduction and first few weeks with caution. The new adult Shar-Pei will need his own stuff in the beginning, and should be kept in a separate area when you aren't around until you know that there won't be any fighting. If your dogs don't have much interest in being the boss and enjoy playing rough, it will take less time for your new Shar-Pei to fit into the pack.

Plan for the introduction to take at least an hour. Since the dogs are all adults, they will need to move at their own pace.

Follow the same steps to introduce your current dogs with your new dog as you would with a puppy.

- Start on neutral territory.
- Have one adult human per dog present at the introduction (this is even more important when introducing an adult canine).
- Introduce one dog at a time – don't let several dogs meet your new Shar-Pei at the same time.

Unlike with a puppy, make sure to bring treats to the meeting of two adult dogs. The animals will respond well to the treats, and you will have a way to quickly distract all of the dogs if they are too tense with each other.

During the introduction, watch the Shar-Pei and your dogs to see if any of them raises his hackles. This is one of the first really obvious signs that a dog is uncomfortable. If the Shar-Pei's hackles are up, back off the introductions for a little bit. Do this by calling your current dog back first. This is also when you should start waving treats around. Avoid pulling on the leashes to separate the dogs. You don't want to add physical tension to the situation because that could trigger a fight. Treats will work for all dogs present in the beginning, and your other dogs should be able to respond to your calling their names.

If any of the dogs are showing their teeth or growling, call your dog back and give the dogs a chance to settle down first. Use the treats and a calming voice to get them to relax. You want all the dogs to feel comfortable during the first meeting, so don't force the friendship. If they seem uncomfortable or wary at first, you will need to let them move at their own pace.

Older Dogs And Your Shar-Pei

If your current dog is older, keep in mind that puppies are energetic and likely to keep trying to engage the older dog in play. This can be very trying for your older canine. Make sure that your older dog isn't getting too tired of the puppy's antics because you don't want your puppy to learn to snap at other dogs. Watch for signs that your older dog is ready for some alone time, some time alone with you, or just a break from the puppy.

Once your Shar-Pei is ready to leave the puppy area for good, you will still want to make sure that your older dog has safe places to go to be alone in case he just doesn't feel up to being around a spry young thing. This will reduce the likelihood that your puppy will be repeatedly scolded and therefore learn to be wary of older dogs.

Even if you adopt an adult Shar-Pei, he can have a lot of energy. This can be a problem with older dogs, so make sure that your dog's golden years aren't marred by a new canine that has rules that don't make sense to your older dog and wants to play in a way your older dog can't.

Photo Courtesy of Ashely Hough

Dog Aggression And Territorial Behaviors

One of the reasons that people adopt a Shar-Pei is to have a dog that will protect them. This can make you feel safe, but it also makes socialization tricky. This is a breed that likes to dominate and be in control. This can be difficult if you already have dogs and cats in the home that are accustomed to a certain type of pecking order.

When people come to visit, you will need to tell them how to interact with your Shar-Pei. Shar-Pei want to protect their pack, and strangers in their territory is definitely a reason to be wary. Do not use choke chains or other negative reinforcers on your Shar-Pei. Not only do those hurt your dog, but a Shar-Pei does not react well to negative reinforcement because he thinks for himself. What you teach your Shar-Pei with these types of restraints is that you don't know what you are doing and are using things to try to force your dog to behave in a certain way. What does work is treats and removal from any negative situation. Reward your dog for the good behavior, and the more often your dog does what you want him to do, the more often you reward him. Chapter 12 discusses how to train your Shar-Pei.

At home, you will need to be more careful. The Shar-Pei is not the kind of dog to back down, so if he feels that someone is challenging him or taking one of his toys, he may react aggressively. While he is young, it is easier to start to train against this kind of behavior, but an older dog will need extra monitoring and should not be left alone with other pets or children. An older Shar-Pei has to learn how to be a part of the pack and the proper way to react to people playing with toys and other items. This is why it is essential to always be firm and consistent.

There are two y types of aggression that you should monitor for in your dog.

- Dominance aggression is when your dog wants to demonstrate control over another animal or person. This kind of aggression is shown through the following behaviors in reaction to anyone going near the Shar-Pei's belongings (like toys or a food bowl):
  - Growling
  - Nipping
  - Snapping

This is the behavior that the pack leader uses to warn others in the pack about touching his stuff. If your Shar-Pei reacts like this toward you, a family member, or another pet going close to his stuff, you must intervene immediately, correct him by saying "No," then lavish him with praise when he stops. You must consistently intervene whenever your Shar-Pei behaves in this manner.

Do not let the Shar-Pei be alone with other people, dogs, or animals as long as any of this type of behavior is exhibited. He will push boundaries, and if you aren't there to intervene, he will likely try to show his dominance in your absence.

You want to train your Shar-Pei not to react aggressively. Once you are sure the behavior has been eliminated, you can leave your dog and Shar-Pei alone for short periods of time, with you staying in another room or somewhere in close proximity, but out of sight. Over time, you can start to leave your pets alone when you go get the mail, then when you run errands. Eventually, you will be able to leave your Shar-Pei alone with other dogs without worrying that he or one of your other dogs will feel compelled to show dominance.

Well socialized males are more interested in meeting and greeting other dogs. Unsocialized males can be aggressive and domineering. Females

*Photo Courtesy
of Allison Christie*

tend to be more predictable; they are more aloof even when properly so-cialized, but they are also less likely to be as aggressive or domineering when they are not socialized.

Your Shar-Pei will have to learn that the home is not just his. It be-longs to people and the other dogs as well, and he is a part of the home, not the boss.

Strong Natural Prey Drive

Over much of the history of the breed, Shar-Pei have chased or fought other animals. After centuries of chasing, they naturally have a high prey drive. If you have small animals, especially cats, this can be a real problem. If you have a cat, we discourage you from adopting an adult Shar-Pei, unless it is absolutely certain that the dog will not chase or potentially kill your cat. You will need to plan to socialize your Shar-Pei puppy with the cat long be-fore the puppy is allowed to run free in the home. Always be present when they interact so that you can correct the puppy's behavior, particularly if the puppy tries to chase the cat.

If you have other small animals, they will need to be kept in areas where your Shar-Pei cannot go. Rabbits, ferrets, and other pets typically are not trainable. Most small animals aren't able to learn not to run away, which your puppy will likely take as an invitation to play. He will likely kill the small animals because that is what centuries of breeding have taught him to do.

This means that you need a high fence – and not an electric one since Shar-Pei will run through it. If you don't have a fence, your dog may be so fo-cused on chasing small creatures that he might run right out into the street. If you have small pets in your home, such as rodents, you will need to keep them in a room or area where your Shar-Pei cannot go at any age. Remem-ber that Shar-Pei are clever and with their height, they can reach a lot of things. Having a door between your dog and smaller animals will be safest thing for everyone.

Feeding Time Practices

Your Shar-Pei puppy will be fed in the puppy space, so mealtime will not be a problem in the beginning. When you start to feed the puppy with the other dogs, you can use the following suggestions to reduce the chance of territorial behavior with food.

STEPS TO ENSURE PEACEFUL EATING

1 ### SIMULTANEOUS BUT SEPARATE FEEDINGS

Feed your Shar-Pei at the same time as the other dogs, but in a different room. Keeping them separated will let your Shar-Pei eat without distractions or feeling that your other dogs will eat what is in his bowl. Make sure to feed your Shar-Pei in the same room each time, while the other dogs eat in their established room or rooms.

2 ### DON'T ALLOW FOOD SHARING

Keep your Shar-Pei and other dogs to their areas until they finish eating their food. Some dogs have a tendency to leave food in the bowl. Don't let them. They need to finish everything in the bowl because all food bowls will be removed as soon as the dogs are done eating.

3 ### STAY NEARBY, BUT DON'T DISTRACT

Make sure you have someone near your Shar-Pei so that he learns not to growl at people near the bowl. This will help to reduce stress when other dogs are around the food. If your dog demonstrates any aggression, immediately correct him by saying "No," then give him praise when he stops. Do not attempt to play with the food bowl, and make sure none of the kids play with it. Your dog needs to know that no one is going to try to steal his food.

4 ### SLOWLY MOVE THE DOGS CLOSER

Move the dogs closer together over a couple of weeks. For example, you can feed your current dog on one side of the door near the doorway and the Shar-Pei on the opposite side near the doorway.

5 ### FINALLY FEED IN THE SAME ROOM

After a month or two, you can feed the dogs in the same room, but with some distance between them. If your Shar-Pei starts to exhibit protective behavior with the other dogs, correct him, then praise him when he stops the behavior.

Eventually, you can start feeding the dogs close together. It can take weeks to months, depending on the age of the Shar-Pei. A puppy will require less time because he will be socialized with the dogs from an early age, making him less wary. That does not mean that he won't display territorial behavior, but it likely won't take long for him to start to feel comfortable eating near the rest of the pack.

For adult dogs, it could take longer, and you should not rush it. Let your dog learn to feel comfortable eating before you make changes, even small ones. Dogs of any breed can be protective of their food, depending on what they have been through; this is exacerbated in protective breeds like the Shar-Pei. Your Shar-Pei needs to feel assured that this protective behavior is not necessary around other dogs before he will eat without incident. That means letting his confidence and comfort build at his own pace.

Photo Courtesy of Lizzie Jennings

CHAPTER 8
The First Few Weeks

"They need to have time to bond to the new family. Lots of snuggles and pets go a long way. We suggest keeping things calm and quiet the first week for the puppy to feel secure and safe with their new family."

Sheila Marquart
Tuck 'N Roll Acres

Photo Courtesy
of Jade Shotton

Sleeping is going to consume most of your Shar-Pei puppy's first week. The rest of the time will see your Shar-Pei puppy yo-yoing between excitement, wariness, and curiosity. When your puppy begins to understand that your home is safe, his personality will start to show, and that is when things will get

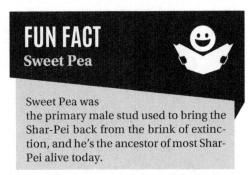

FUN FACT
Sweet Pea

Sweet Pea was the primary male stud used to bring the Shar-Pei back from the brink of extinction, and he's the ancestor of most Shar-Pei alive today.

interesting. A Shar-Pei's intellect often shows as curiosity, and that means you are going to need to keep an eye on your pup. They are also incredibly goofy once they get comfortable, and that is what really makes them such an ideal pet.

At this time, you will also need to begin socialization (once the shots are completed) and training. If the breeder has already started housetraining, you definitely want to keep using their method from the moment you get your pup home. It should not be a long struggle since Shar-Pei like to keep their area clean – but make it a bit easier on yourself and your dog by keeping any existing momentum going.

The bond you start to build in the first week will continue to develop over the first month. By the end of the first month, your pup should be sleeping through the night and may have a fairly good understanding of where to go to the bathroom. You will also have a pretty good understanding of your canine's personality, which will make it a lot easier to know how to comfort the puppy during his infrequent bouts of uncertainty.

The first month is when you really need to start paying attention to your puppy's emerging personality. Like with all intelligent breeds, when it comes to training, the key during this time is to remain consistent; that means everyone, not just the person who is the favorite. Use what you learn about your puppy's personality to encourage good behavior.

Setting The Rules And Sticking To Them

Your puppy needs to understand the rules and know that you and your family mean them. Once your canine learns to listen to you, there will probably still be times when he isn't going to want to listen – but he'll be much more likely to listen when he knows you are in control. Shar-Pei can be incredibly stubborn. No matter how cute your Shar-Pei is, for your sake and his, you need to let him know who is boss in a way that is firm, but not threatening.

Photo Courtesy
of Vannity Monroid

Establish A No Jumping And No Mouthing Policy

If not properly trained, Shar-Pei will bite children when they are afraid. It's your responsibility to ensure that your dog learns how to play properly, which means not jumping up on people or nipping them. Between their natural instincts and dental problems, it is also best to avoid playing tug-of-war. Any games that involve biting or nipping should always be avoided.

Nipping

- One of the triggers for nipping is overstimulation, which can be one of the signs that your puppy is too tired to keep playing or training and you should put him to bed.

- Another trigger could be that your canine has too much energy. If this is the case, take your puppy outside to burn off some of his excess energy. At the same time, be careful not to over-exercise the puppy.

You need to be vigilant and immediately let your puppy know that nipping is not acceptable. Some people recommend using a water spritzer bottle and spraying the puppy while saying "No" after nipping. This is one of the few times when punishment may be effective, but you need to be careful that your dog doesn't associate it with anything other than the nipping.

Always tell your puppy "No" firmly whenever he is nipping, even if it is during playtime. You should also pull away and say "Ouch!" loudly to let your puppy know that his teeth are hurting you. This will help to establish the idea that nipping is bad and is never rewarded.

Chewing

All puppies chew to relieve the pain of teething. Chewing can be an expensive problem for your dog to have, but it is fairly common with this breed. Whether he is chewing your furniture, utensils, or clothing, you want to discourage this behavior as quickly as possible.

- Make sure you have toys for your Shar-Pei (whether adult or puppy) so that you can teach him what things are acceptable to chew on. Having a lot of available toys, and rotating those toys out, will help give your puppy or dog a variety of options.

- If your puppy is teething, either refrigerate a couple of toys so they are cold, or give your puppy frozen carrots. The cold will help to numb the pain.

- Toys that are made either of hard rubber or hard nylon are best, particularly Kongs with kibble in them. You can even fill them with wa-

Photo Courtesy of Chelsey Gates

ter and freeze them, which will give your puppy something cool to soothe the pain of teething.

For the most part, keeping your eye on your dog when he is not in his designated space will help you to quickly see when he is chewing on things he shouldn't. When this happens, say "No" firmly. If your dog continues to chew, put him back in his space. While he is in the space, make sure he has plenty of toys to chew on.

If you decide to use chew deterrents, such as different bitter and training sprays, be aware that some dogs will not care that an item tastes bad – they will chew anyway. Do not apply these deterrents and then leave your dog alone and expect him to just stop chewing. You need to see your dog's reaction before trusting that the bad habit is broken. Since some Shar-Pei can have separation anxiety, you will definitely want to find a way to alleviate the problem with chewing as quickly as possible so that your pup can be free to roam around your home.

Jumping

Dogs typically jump up on people when they first greet them. Use the following steps when you have a visitor (and if you can get someone who is willing to help, because that will make the training that much easier).

6 STEPS TO ELIMINATING JUMPING UP ON VISITORS

1 PUT A LEASH ON THE DOG
when the person knocks on the door or rings the bell. The arrival of someone else will invariably excite most dogs, especially puppies.

2 LET THE PERSON IN
but do not approach the person with the puppy until he calms down.

3 REINFORCE PROPER BEHAVIOR WITH PRAISE
when the puppy keeps all four paws on the ground. Approach the visitor only after your Shar-Pei is calm.

4 IGNORE INCORRECT BEHAVIOR
Turn your body and ignore him when the puppy jumps up. Don't verbally correct him. Being completely ignored will be far more of a deterrent than any words you can say.

5 USE DISTRACTIONS TO HELP THEM CALM DOWN
Give your dog something to hold in his mouth if he does not settle down. Sometimes dogs just need a task to reduce their excitement. A stuffed animal or ball are ideal for distraction, even if your dog drops it.

6 GET LOW AND PET YOUR DOG
Having someone on his level will make him feel like he is being included. It also lets him sniff your face, which is part of a proper greeting. If your visitor is willing to help, this obvious acknowledgment can be a deterrent from jumping as the person is already on your dog's level.

Reward-Based Training Vs. Discipline-Based Training

"While they do require some discipline, most respond to correction easily due to their desire to please. Shar-pei require an owner who is a leader. If they do not receive early guidance they will quickly take over. A new owner should expect a few challenges along the way, but with a firm upbringing, a lifetime devoted companion."

Debbie Raynor
DC Shar-pei

Photo Courtesy of Laur Dyck

Other chapters detail the various aspects of training, but it is important to keep in mind just how much more efficient it is to train with rewards than with punishments, especially for an intelligent breed like the Shar-Pei. This will be a particular challenge as puppies can be exuberant and are easily distracted. It is important to remember that your puppy is young, so you need to keep your temper and learn when you need to take a break from training.

Several critical aspects that you will need to start working on during the first month:

- Housetraining (Chapter 9)

- Crate training (Chapter 6)

- Barking (Chapter 11)

Find out how much the breeder did in terms of housetraining and other such areas. The best breeders may even teach puppies one or two commands before the puppy goes home with you. If this is the case, keep using those same commands with your puppy so that the early training is not lost. This can help you establish the right tone of voice to use since the puppy will already know what the words mean and how to react to them.

Separation Anxiety In Dogs And Puppies

Shar-Pei are not known for being prone to separation anxiety, likely because they are more independent dogs. However, that doesn't mean it is guaranteed that your dog will always be fine. If your Shar-Pei does have separation anxiety, he can do a lot of damage. You will want to plan to help your new dog know that everything will be just fine, even if you have to leave him alone for hours. Apart from making sure your dog is tired before you leave home, there are several ways you can prepare your puppy or dog for those longer days when he is left home alone.

In the beginning, keep the puppy's time alone to a minimum. The sounds of people moving around the house will help your Shar-Pei understand that the separation is not permanent. After the first week or so, alone time can involve you going out to get the mail, leaving the puppy inside by himself for just a few minutes. You can then lengthen the amount of time you are away from the puppy over a few days until the puppy is alone for 30 minutes or so at a time.

Here are some basic guidelines for when you first start to leave your puppy alone.

- Take the puppy out about 30 minutes before you leave.

- Tire the puppy out with exercise or playtime so that your leaving is not such a big deal.

- Place the puppy in the puppy area well ahead of when you go out to avoid having him associate the space with something bad happening.

- Don't give your puppy extra attention right before you leave because that reinforces the idea that you give attention before something bad happens.

- Avoid reprimanding your Shar-Pei for any bad behavior that happens while you are away. Reprimanding teaches him to be more stressed because it will seem like you come home angry.

If your Shar-Pei exhibits signs of separation anxiety, there are several things you can do to help make him comfortable during your absence.

- Chew toys can give your dog something acceptable to gnaw on while you are away.

- A blanket or shirt that smells like you or other family members can help provide comfort too. If you have worn the item and haven't gotten it very dirty, this is ideal, just make sure that you were not in contact with any chemicals over the course of the day you wore it. You also need to make sure that your dog won't eat the item in your absence. Consider giving him something that you know you won't wear again, in case he shreds it to pieces.

- Leave the area well lit, even if it is during the day. Should something happen and you get home later than you intended to, you don't want your little guy to be in the dark.

- Turn on a stereo (classical music is best) or television (old-timey shows that don't have loud noises, like Mr. Ed or I Love Lucy, work best) so that the house isn't completely quiet and unfamiliar noises are less obvious.

It will not take your Shar-Pei long to notice the kind of behaviors that indicate you are leaving. Grabbing your keys, purse, wallet, and other indications will quickly become triggers that can make your Shar-Pei anxious because he'll quickly learn what these actions mean. Don't make a big deal out of it. If you act in a normal way, over time this will help your little one to understand that your leaving is fine and that everything will be all right.

How Long Is Too Long To Be Left Home Alone?

You should not leave your dog home alone for more than eight hours at a time. He will likely be all right between four and eight hours, but any longer than that and he may start to have problems. Though the breed is often independent, they are still pack animals. They do better when they have their pack than when they are left home alone for long periods of time.

Photo Courtesy of Megan Yiu

One of the problems in the beginning is that your dog will need to be in a crate, and that means he will be crated for the entire time you are gone. Initially, this time should be very short. As your dog becomes housetrained and more trustworthy, your goal should be to allow your dog to be out of the crate so that it doesn't feel like a punishment. Your companion will not do well being trapped in a crate for hours at a time. You need to find some good mental games or things that your pup can do while you are gone. This is also why it is vital to ensure that you have your home properly prepared prior to your dog's arrival, especially if you get an adult Shar-Pei. Once your dog is crate trained and you start trying to leave him alone for longer periods of time, you want to make sure any destructive urges are put in check as much as possible.

Photo Courtesy of Mitch Keller

Don't Overdo It, Physically Or Mentally

A tired puppy is a lot like a tired toddler; you have to keep the little guy from becoming exhausted or overworking those little legs. You need to be careful about harming your puppy's growing bones. Your pup is probably going to think that sleep is unnecessary, no matter how tired he is. It is up to you to read the signs that tell you when to stop all activities and put your pup to bed or take a break.

Training needs to be conducted in increments of time that your puppy or dog can handle. Be careful that you aren't pushing the training past the puppy's concentration threshold or that you aren't discouraging your adult dog with commands that are too advanced for him. If you continue training past your puppy's energy levels, the lessons learned are not going to be the ones you want to teach your dog. At this age, training sessions don't need to be long, they just need to be consistent.

Walks will be much shorter during that first month. When you go out, stay within a few blocks of home. Don't worry – by the month's end, your puppy will have a lot more stamina so you can enjoy longer walks and short trips away from home if needed. You can also do a bit of walking on the leash in the yard if your puppy has a lot of extra energy. This will help your Shar-Pei learn how to behave on the leash. Puppies have a tendency to want to attack the leash because it is a distraction from running freely. Moderate exercise during the cool parts of the day is fine, but you should not be jogging with any brachial breed, including the Shar-Pei.

Just because your puppy can't take long walks initially doesn't mean that he won't have plenty of energy. Daily exercise will be essential, with the caveat that you need to make sure your puppy isn't doing too much, too soon. Staying active will help him to not only be healthy, but keep him mentally stimulated. You will quickly realize just how sedentary you have been if you have never had a dog before because you will be on the move almost all of the time the puppy is awake.

CHAPTER 9
Housetraining

"Fortunately, Shar-pei are easily house trained. Most housebreak themselves. They are highly intelligent and quickly learn what is expected of them. Puppy meals should be scheduled. Take them out to potty within 30 minutes of eating. In between meals, watch for clues that they may need to go out. Whining, circling, and coming to you repeatedly are all signs they may need to relieve themselves."

Debbie Raynor
DC Shar-pei

Photo Courtesy
of Allison Valentine

Housetraining a puppy isn't really any more difficult or time consuming than potty training a toddler, and with a Shar-Pei, it is actually a bit easier. It is important to set a schedule and then not deviate from it. Your new family member will want a clean area and will quickly learn to let you know when he needs to go. The fact that Shar-Pei prefer a clean environment is definitely something you should be using to your advantage.

Photo Courtesy of Pedro Lopez

Using a leash can be helpful in ensuring that your puppy learns when and where to go, but there will still be challenges as you try to convince your puppy that there is a designated place to use the bathroom and it isn't in your home.

Make sure to consistently apply these two rules.

1. Never let the puppy roam the home alone – he should always be in his dedicated puppy space when you aren't watching him. Your Shar-Pei won't like a soiled crate, so that is a deterrent from doing his business when you are not around. He may not take the same approach to other areas of the home if he is left free to wander.

2. Give your puppy constant, easy access to the locations where you plan to housetrain him. You will need to make frequent trips outside as your puppy learns where to do his business, particularly if constant access to a place to use the restroom isn't possible. When you go out, put a leash on your puppy to make a point of where in the yard you want him to use the bathroom.

Always begin with a training plan, then be even stricter with yourself than you are with your puppy to keep that schedule. You are the key to the puppy learning where it is acceptable to do his business.

Easy If Your Dog Knows You're The Boss

Intelligent, independent breeds like the Shar-Pei require a firm, consistent approach right from the beginning. They have to learn who is in charge, otherwise they will not want to listen to you later. Fortunately, positive reinforcements and treats will do wonders to help you in the beginning. Keeping a firm hand will ensure that your Shar-Pei learns his place in the hierarchy.

Training can be even easier if the breeder has already started the training. Just make sure you know what the breeder was doing so that you can pick up from where they stopped. This is an incredibly intelligent breed that is predisposed to cleanliness. Getting over one of the worst parts of training can be a near breeze if you are kind, consistent, and firm.

Photo Courtesy of Colin and Jeannette Simmons

Inside Or Outside – Housetraining Options And Considerations

If you were lucky enough to find a breeder who has already started the housetraining process, make sure to coordinate with them early so you can start from the same place. Without a break in the training, your Shar-Pei will be housetrained far faster than most dogs.

You have the following housetraining options for your puppy:

- **Pee pads** – You should have several around the home for training, including in the puppy's area, but as far from his bed as possible.

- **Regular outings outside** – Organize these based on your puppy's sleeping and eating schedule.

- **Rewards** – You can use treats in the beginning, but quickly shift to praise.

In the beginning, the best way to housetrain your dog is to go out a lot of times, including at night, so that your puppy learns to keep all of his business outside. During the first few months, it is best to use a leash when you take the puppy out. This will help him learn to walk on a leash and keep him from getting distracted before he does his business.

A word of warning – don't start praising the puppy until he's done going to the bathroom. Interrupting him in mid-potty may make the puppy stop, increasing the odds that he will go again after you get back inside.

Setting A Schedule

You need to keep an eye on your puppy and consistently have housetraining sessions:

- After eating

- After waking up from sleeping or each nap

- On a schedule (after it has been established)

One of the most important things you can do is to watch your Shar-Pei for cues like sniffing and circling, two common activities as a puppy searches for a place to go. Start tailoring your schedule around your puppy's unique needs.

Puppies have small bladders and little control in the early days. If you have to initially train your pup to do his business inside, there needs to be a single designated space with a clean pee pad in the puppy's area, and you

Photo Courtesy
of Junairah Dipatuan & Raymond Lopez

need to stock up on the appropriate pads for the puppy. Then make sure you change those pads regularly so your puppy does not get accustomed to having waste nearby. Pee pads are better than newspaper and can absorb more. Even if you use pads, you will still need to plan to transition to having the dog do his business outdoors as quickly as possible.

Choosing A Location

A designated restroom space can help make the experience of house-training easier because your Shar-Pei will begin to associate one area of the yard for that one purpose, rather than sniffing around until he finds a choice spot. Having him go in one spot regularly will also make cleanup much simpler too; that way you can continue to use the whole yard instead of having to worry about stepping in waste.

Given how much Shar-Pei love to dig, you should probably place the designated bathroom area away from any fences. Shar-Pei can be very particular about weather, so having the designated area close to the door and under some kind of protection will greatly encourage your dog to always go outside – instead of pottying inside because he doesn't want to be out in the inclement weather.

When you are out for walks is the perfect time to train your puppy to go to the bathroom. Between walks and the yard, your puppy will come to see the leash as a sign that it is time to relieve his bladder, which could become a Pavlovian response.

Make sure that you pay attention to your puppy the entire time you are outside. You need to make sure that he understands the purpose of going outside is to go to the bathroom. Do not send your puppy outside alone and assume that he's done what you wanted him to do. Until there are no more accidents in the home, you need to verify that your puppy isn't losing focus while he is outside.

Keyword Training

All training should include keywords, even housetraining. You and all members of the family should know what words to use when training your dog where to go to the bathroom, and you should all be using those words consistently. If you have paired an adult with a child, the adult should be the one using the keyword during training.

To avoid confusing your puppy, be careful not to select words that you often use inside the home. Use a phrase like "Get busy" to let your puppy know it's time to get to work, not something that involves the word "bathroom" or "potty"– these are words that you will likely say in casual conversation, which could trigger your dog to go when he's not supposed to. "Get busy" is not a phrase most people use in their daily routine, so it is not something you are likely to say when you don't mean for your puppy to use the bathroom.

Once your puppy learns to use the bathroom based on the command, make sure he finishes before offering praise or rewards.

*Photo Courtesy
of Jerad Cook*

Reward Good Behavior With Positive Reinforcement

Positive reinforcement is very effective. In the beginning, take a few pieces of kibble with you when you are teaching your puppy where to go, both inside and outside the home. Learning that you are the one in charge will help teach your Shar-Pei to look to you for cues and instructions.

Part of being consistent with training means lavishing the little guy with praise whenever your puppy does the right thing. If you gently lead your puppy to his bathroom area on a leash without any other stops, it will gradually become obvious that your Shar-Pei should go there to use the bathroom. Once you get outside, encourage your pup to go when you get to the place in the yard that is intended to be his bathroom spot. As soon as he does his business, give him immediate and very enthusiastic praise. Pet your puppy as you talk to let the little guy know just how good the action was. Once the praise is done, return inside immediately. This is not playtime. You want your puppy to associate certain outings with designated potty time.

While praise is far more effective for Shar-Pei, you can also give your puppy a treat after a few successful trips outside. Definitely do not make treats a habit after each trip because you do not want your Shar-Pei to expect one every time he does his business. The lesson is to go outside, and the puppy can learn that such outings may include treats.

The best way to housetrain in the first month or two is to go out every hour or two, even at night. You will need to set an alarm to wake you within that time to take the puppy outside. Use the leash to keep the focus on using the bathroom, give the same enthusiastic praise, then immediately return inside and go to bed. It is difficult, but your Shar-Pei will get the hang of it a lot faster if there isn't a long period between potty breaks. Over time, the pup will need to go outside less frequently, giving you more rest.

If your Shar-Pei has an accident, it is important to refrain from punishing the puppy. Accidents are not a reason to punish – it really reflects more on your training and schedule than on the puppy. That said, accidents are pretty much an inevitability. When it happens, tell your puppy, "No. Potty outside!" and clean up the mess immediately. Once that is done take the puppy outside to go potty. Of course, if your puppy doesn't go, he doesn't get any praise.

Photo Courtesy
of Lisa & Rob Farr

Cleaning Up

Clean up any messes in the home as soon as you find them. Unless you catch your puppy using the bathroom in the home, there is no point in negative reinforcement. Your dog will simply learn to hide his mess to avoid being punished. Take the dog outside instead and see if he will use the bathroom. If someone is home, it is best to clean up the mess as quickly as possible. Spend a bit of time researching what kinds of cleaner you want to use, whether generic or holistic. For example, you will likely want to get a product with an enzyme cleaner. Enzymes help to remove stains by speeding up the chemical reaction of the cleaner with the stain. They also help to remove the smell faster, reducing the odds that your dog will continue to go to the bathroom in the same place. Shar-Pei don't have an issue with marking their territory, especially if they are properly trained, but you want to discourage dogs that are visiting from claiming areas where your puppy has had accidents.

HELPFUL TIP
Crate Training

While you may not plan on keeping your adult Shar-Pei in a crate, all puppies should be crate trained. While it helps with house-training, the biggest reason to crate train your Shar-Pei puppy is that he will likely encounter a crate or kennel at a groomer, vet, or boarding facility at some point in his life. If your dog doesn't learn to become comfortable in a crate as a puppy, fear can cause the dog to hurt himself trying to escape one as an adult.

Pay attention to when these accidents happen and determine if there is a commonality between them. Perhaps you need to add an additional trip outside for your puppy or should make a change in his walking schedule. Or maybe there is something that is startling your dog, causing an accident.

CHAPTER 10
Socialization

"Socialization should begin early, as soon as the puppy vaccines are completed. I would begin by socializing with dogs you know, like pets of friends, ones you are aware of their temperament. The AKC also offers supervised puppy classes. I would caution against dog parks until your puppy is socialized and you are confident he will behave appropriately around other dogs."

Debbie Raynor
DC Shar-pei

Photo Courtesy
of Josie Buffo

The Shar-Pei is a loyal, noble breed of dog that loves to be with familiar people, but is much more wary of strangers. When not properly socialized, Shar-Pei can suffer from anxiety and fear, which will make them more aggressive towards other dogs. Also, a poorly socialized Shar-Pei is more likely to escape, even if that seems counterintuitive. Because he is a member of your family, you want your Shar-Pei to be happy around other people and dogs and to learn that the vast majority of them are not a threat to you or your home.

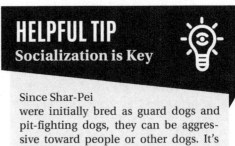

HELPFUL TIP
Socialization is Key

Since Shar-Pei were initially bred as guard dogs and pit-fighting dogs, they can be aggressive toward people or other dogs. It's crucial to introduce them to as many people, dogs, and places as possible when they are young puppies to prevent aggressive behavior later.

Socialization allows your Shar-Pei puppy to learn that it can be a lot of fun to play with people you invite into your home and dogs that you encounter out on your walks. To make sure your Shar-Pei is comfortable, you have to plan to start socialization from a very early age.

Remember that your puppy will need to have all of his vaccinations before being exposed to other dogs.

Socialization Can Make Life Easier In The Long Run

All dogs need socialization, but intelligent breeds have more analytical minds, so you want them to learn as early as possible that most of the time the world is a safe place and that other people and animals usually don't pose a threat. It will also help for your puppy to learn that acting in a dominant, aggressive way is not acceptable.

The benefit of early socialization is that it can make life that much more enjoyable for everyone involved, no matter what the situation is. A socialized dog will approach the world from a much better place than a dog that is not socialized.

Greeting New People

"Puppy classes work very well with the Shar Pei. You can also take them to Home Depot, Lowes, Petco, Petsmart. While they are pupies, let everyone touch them and praise them when they are good."

Lynn Olds
Lava Kennels

Puppies will likely enjoy meeting new people, so make sure to invite people over to help socialize your canine family member. To introduce your puppy to a new person, try one of these methods:

1. Try to have your puppy meet new people daily, if possible. This could be during walks or while you are doing other activities when you get out of the house. If you can't meet new people daily, try for at least 4 times a week.

Photo Courtesy of Angharad White

Photo Courtesy
of Stephanie Michel-Fife

2. Invite friends and family over, and let them spend a few minutes just giving the puppy attention. If your puppy has a favorite game or activity, let people know so that they can play with him. This will win the little guy over very quickly and teach him that new people are fun and safe to be with.

3. Once your puppy is old enough to learn tricks (after the first month – don't try to teach him tricks immediately; he needs a bit more time and you will need to see if his personality is a good fit for tricks), have your little friend demonstrate the tricks for visitors. This will be really important because a lot of people are nervous around dogs of any size.

4. Avoid crowds for the first few months. When your puppy is several months to a year old, attend some dog-friendly events so that your pup can learn not to be uncomfortable around a large group of people.

Greeting New Dogs

Chapter 7 covers the introduction of your new Shar-Pei with your other dogs, but meeting dogs that aren't part of your home is a little different, especially since you can encounter them when you are out walking. You need to train your Shar-Pei as early as possible because you will want to be able to walk around your neighborhood without your dog becoming aggressive. Most dogs will bow and sniff each other during an introduction. Watch for

Photo Courtesy of Chelsey Gates

the same signs of aggression covered in Chapter 7, such as raised hackles and bared teeth. Bowing, high tail, and perked ears usually mean that your Shar-Pei is excited about meeting the dog. If your Shar-Pei is making noises, watch for the signs of aggression to make sure that the sounds are playful, not uneasy.

According to the Shar-Pei Society, about a third of Shar-Pei have been reported to be aggressive toward other dogs (none of them are aggressive to people). If your Shar-Pei is aggressive, you want to train him early so that this isn't an issue. The best way to do that is with playdates in a neutral place. This will remove any jealousy about sharing toys or territorial tendencies.

Don't let your Shar-Pei jump up on other dogs. If he does, immediately say "No," to let him know that is not acceptable behavior. This can become a way of showing dominance, which you really don't want with your pup, even if it is just play in the beginning.

The Importance Of Continuing Socialization

Even friendly dogs need to be socialized. This doesn't mean you should force your puppy into interaction, but joining classes and setting up playdates will give your dog a reason to be excited about meeting other dogs.

Have family and friends visit regularly, bringing any dogs along, so that your Shar-Pei has constant reminders that his home is a welcoming place, not somewhere that he needs to exert his dominance. You don't want your pup to feel that the outside world is fine, but that he can be a terror at home.

Socializing An Adult Dog

Sometimes an adult dog will be too set in his ways to change, particularly if your dog is in his golden years. However, most adult dogs can be socialized as long as you make it your top priority (along with training). If you aren't prepared to be very patient with your Shar-Pei adult, then it is best not to adopt an adult. There is a chance that your Shar-Pei won't be as friendly with other dogs, even if he seems to be all right with other dogs at the rescue facility. Before you can begin to socialize your dog, you need to make sure he already knows some basic commands and that you have him under control before any introductions are made.

Photo Courtesy of Malin Edmark

Socializing an adult canine requires a lot of time, dedication, gentle training, and a firm approach. You may be lucky enough to get an adult that is already well socialized. However, that does not mean that you can be entirely relaxed. The dog may have had a bad experience with a particular breed of dog that no one knows about.

***

If you have problems with your adult dog, consult a behaviorist or specialized trainer. For instance, if you have to avoid dogs during that first week because your Shar-Pei is not reacting well to them, a professional will help you learn how to better socialize your adult dog.

120

TIPS FOR CONTINUED SOCIALIZATION

TIP 1

MASTER THE BASIC COMMANDS

Your dog should be adept at the following commands before you work on socialization: *Sit, Down, Heel, Stay.* Stay is especially important because if your dog can remain in one place based on your commands, then he is demonstrating self-control, something that will be very helpful for socialization because you can override an aggressive impulse by activating the listening mode. When you go outside, you will need to be very aware of your surroundings, and be able to command your dog before another dog or person gets near.

TIP 2

USE A SHORT LEASH ON WALKS

At the first sign of aggression, turn and walk in the opposite direction. Being aware of your surroundings will start to cue you into what your dog is reacting to so you can start training your dog not to react negatively.

TIP 3

CHANGE DIRECTION

if you notice that your Shar-Pei is not reacting well to a particular person or dog approaching you. Avoidance is a good short term solution until you know that your dog is more accepting of the presence of these other dogs or people.

If you aren't able to take a different direction, tell your dog to sit, then block your dog's view. This can prove to be very challenging as your dog will try to look around you. Engage in training to get your dog to listen to you, taking his mind off of what is coming toward him.

TIP 4

SCHEDULE PLAY DATES WITH FRIENDLY DOGS

Ask friends with friendly dogs to visit you, then meet in an enclosed space. Having one or two friendly dogs interact with your dog can help your Shar-Pei to see that not all dogs are dangerous or need to be put in their place. Having the dogs walk around the area together without a lot of interaction can help your dog learn that other dogs are usually just interested in enjoying the outside, so there is no reason to try to bully them.

TIP 5

GET SPECIAL TREATS JUST FOR WALKS

If your dog is aggressive when walking, have him sit, and give him one of the special treats. Shar-Pei are food motivated, so this could be a perfect way of distracting your dog from whatever is making him feel protective. At the first snarl or sign of aggression, engage the training mentality and draw upon your dog's desire for those special treats. This method is slow, but it is reliable over time because your dog is learning that the appearance of strangers and other dogs means special treats, a positive experience, not a negative one. However, this does not train the dog to interact with those dogs. You can couple it with the fourth suggestion to get the best results.

CHAPTER 11
Training Your Shar-Pei

"The Shar Pei is a very intelligent breed. When I was doing obedience with my dogs, the trainer would always ask how long I worked with them. But to be honest, I actually worked with my dog's way less than the others were worked with."

Lynn Olds
Lava Kennels

Photo Courtesy
of Jemma Chase

The breed's intelligence means that your Shar-Pei is going to quickly pick up on what you are trying to teach him. However, before your Shar-Pei will do what he's told, he has to know that he isn't the boss, and that is really where your first lessons need to focus. Making sure your dog understands who is alpha isn't about being mean or making the dog fear you – that's not how you train a dog. You want him to feel like he is a part of the family, so take a similar approach as when you teach a toddler that listening is mandatory. Unlike with a toddler though, once a Shar-Pei learns that you are in charge, you don't have to deal with things like teenage rebellion. In fact, he may help you keep others in line.

He will love the attention, but there may be times when your dog just doesn't feel like listening, no matter what bribe you offer. This is one reason to always be careful about how many treats you give your Shar-Pei (the other reason being the risk of your dog becoming overweight or obese).

Shar-Pei can be fantastic to train for many types of skills. They love playing, they love being around you, though they may feel that training is more about training you – they want treats or toys, so they are willing to do what you ask in order to "make you" give them the treats or toys. Their natural enthusiasm for doing new things and spending time with their people is all they need to make them happy. Their stubbornness can occasionally make it a bit more of a challenge, but keep your cool.

While training will get increasingly more enjoyable over time, it will likely be slow going in the beginning as your dog will be quite excited for the interaction. You will need to be firm and consistent, as well as keeping the training sessions very short in the beginning. If you are patient with your pup from the start, you will find that it will pay off later.

Benefits Of Proper Training

In addition to making socialization and general excursions easier, training could be a way of saving your dog's life. Understanding commands will help to stop your dog from running into the street or from responding to provocations from other dogs (or from acting as the aggressor). Training could also be a time saver in the event your dog gets away from you.

Training is a great way to bond with your dog. It gives you dedicated time together and helps you to understand your puppy's developing personality and to learn what kinds of rewards will work best for other tasks, like socialization. This is a dog that can join you when you go out for picnics or on other outings, so you want to make sure your Shar-Pei is trained so that you can enjoy a full range of activities.

Choosing The Right Reward

"Shar-Pei love to please their owners and do great with learning obedience or tricks. However, they do get bored easily so keep your exciting and reward with plenty of praise and treats."

Janet Saporito
Thornapple Hill Chinese Shar-Pei

Photo Courtesy of June Juul Nielsen

The right reward for a Shar-Pei will ultimately be love and affection. Treats are the easiest way of keying a puppy into the idea that performing tricks is a good behavior. Soon, though, you will need to switch to a reward that is a secondary reinforcer. Praise, additional playtime, and extra petting are all fantastic rewards for your Shar-Pei. Your dog will probably follow you around until you decide to just sit back and relax. Plopping down to watch a movie and letting your puppy sit with you is a great reward after an intense training session. Not only did your puppy learn, but you both now get to relax together.

Remember, this is a breed that is prone to obesity, which can be detrimental to your dog's health. Make sure that you switch to a different kind of positive reward as early as possible. Shar-Pei love their toys too, so you don't have to solely rely on praise (something that may or may not be a good reward depending on your dog's mood or preferences).

If you would like your Shar-Pei to attach positive feedback with a sound, you can use a clicker. They are relatively inexpensive and need to be used at the same time as you praise your puppy or dog. Clickers are not necessary, but some trainers find them useful.

Name Recognition

Over time, many of us come up with multiple names for our dogs. Nicknames, joke names, and descriptions based on some of their ridiculous actions (it's why we love them) can all be used later. However, before you can train a dog, you have to make sure he understands his real name.

1. Get some treats and show one to your dog.
2. Say the dog's name, immediately say "Yes" (your dog should be looking at you when you speak), then give your dog a treat.
3. Wait 10 seconds, then show your dog a treat and repeat step 2.

Sessions shouldn't last longer than about five minutes because your dog will lose focus or interest. Name recognition is something you can do several times over the day. After you have done this over five to ten sessions, the training will change a bit.

1. Wait until your dog isn't paying attention to you.
2. Call your dog. If he has a leash on, give it a gentle tug to get your dog's attention.
3. Say "Yes" and give the dog a treat when he looks at you.

During this time, do not speak your dog's name during corrections or for no real reason. This is because in the beginning, you need to get the dog to associate the name only with something very positive, like treats. This will more quickly program your dog to listen to you no matter what else is going on around him.

It is likely that your Shar-Pei will not require a lot of time before he recognizes his name.

Essential Commands

"The basic commands for any dog are essential. Start with sit, stay, and come. These will be useful forever and are so necessary because someday that cute puppy will be a 50-60 lb. adult!"

Kathleen Probst
Conrad Knoll Chinese Shar-Pei

Photo Courtesy of Charlemagne Fezza

There are five basic commands that all dogs should know. These commands are the basis for a happy and enjoyable relationship with your dog. By the time your puppy learns all five of the commands, the correlation between the words you say and the expected actions will be more obvious. This will clue the dog in to understanding new words in terms of expectation and will make it much easier to train him on the more complex concepts.

Train your puppy to do the commands in the order they appear in this chapter. Sit is a basic command, and something all dogs already naturally do. Since dogs sit often, it is the easiest command to teach. Teaching leave it and drop it is much more difficult, and it usually requires that the puppy fight an instinct or desire. Consider how much you give in to something you want to do when you know you shouldn't – that's pretty much what you are facing, but with a puppy. Quiet can be another difficult command as dogs (particularly puppies) tend to bark as a natural reaction to something – fortunately with Shar-Pei this is almost certainly not going to be a problem.

Here are some basic guidelines to follow during training.

- Include everyone in the home in the Shar-Pei training. The puppy must learn to listen to everyone in the household, and not just one or two people. A set training schedule may only involve a couple of people in the beginning, especially if you have children. There should always be an adult present for training, but including one child during training will help reinforce the idea that the puppy must listen to everyone in the house. It is also a good way for a parent to monitor a child's interaction with the puppy so that everyone plays in a way that is safe and follows the rules.

- To get started, select an area where you and your puppy have no other distractions, including noise. Leave your phone and other devices out of range so that you keep your attention on the puppy.

- Stay happy and excited about the training. Your puppy will pick up on your enthusiasm, and will focus better because of it.

- Be consistent and firm as you teach.

- Bring a special treat to the first few training sessions, such as pieces of chicken or small treats.

Sit

Start to teach sit when your puppy is around eight weeks old. Once you settle into your quiet training location:

1. Hold out a treat.

2. Move the treat over your puppy's head. This will make the puppy move back.

3. Say "sit" as the puppy's haunches touch the floor.

Having a second person around to demonstrate this with your puppy will be helpful as they can sit to show what you mean.

Wait until your puppy starts to sit down and say sit as he sits. If your puppy finishes sitting down, give praise. Naturally, this will make your puppy incredibly excited and wiggly, so it may take a bit of time before he will want to sit again. When the time comes and the puppy starts to sit again, repeat the process.

It's going to take more than a couple of sessions for the puppy to fully connect your words with the actions. Commands are something completely new to your little companion. Once your puppy has demonstrated mastery over sit, start teaching down.

Down

Repeat the same process to teach this command as you did for sit.

1. Tell your dog to sit.

2. Hold out the treat.

3. Lower the treat to the floor with your dog sniffing at it. Allow your pup to lick the treat, but if he stands up, start over.

4. Say down as the puppy's elbows touch the floor, then give praise while letting your puppy eat the treat.

Wait until the puppy starts to lie down, then say down. If the Shar-Pei finishes the action, offer your chosen reward.

It will probably take a little less time to teach this command.

Wait until your puppy has mastered down before moving on to stay.

Stay

Stay is a vital command to teach because it can keep your puppy from running across a street or from running at someone who is nervous or scared of dogs. It is important that your dog has mastered sit and down before you teach stay. Learning this command is going to be more difficult since it isn't something that your puppy does naturally. Be prepared for it to take a bit longer.

1. Tell your puppy to either sit or stay.

2. As you do this, place your hand in front of the puppy's face.

3. Wait until the puppy stops trying to lick your hand before you begin again.

4. When the puppy settles down, take a step away. If your puppy is not moving, say stay and give a treat and some praise.

Giving your puppy the reward indicates that the command is over, but you also need to indicate that the command is complete. The puppy has to learn to stay until you say it is okay to leave the spot. Once you give the okay to move, do not give treats. Come should not be used as the okay word as it is a command used for something else.

Repeat these steps, taking more steps further from the puppy after a successful command.

Once your puppy understands stay when you move away, start training to stay even if you are not moving. Extend the amount of time required for the puppy to stay in one spot so that he understands that stay ends with the okay command.

When you feel that your puppy has stay mastered, start training the puppy to come.

Come

This is a command you can't teach until the puppy has learned the previous commands. Before you start the training session, decide if you want to use come or come here for the command. Be consistent in the words you use.

This command is important for the same reason as the previous one. If you are around people who are nervous around dogs, or encounter a wild animal or other distraction, this command can snap your puppy's attention back to you.

1. Leash the puppy.

2. Tell the puppy to stay.

3. Move away from the puppy.

4. Say the command you will use for come and give a gentle tug on the leash toward you.

Repeat these steps, building a larger distance between you and the puppy. Once the puppy seems to understand it, remove the leash and start at a close distance. If your puppy doesn't seem to understand the command, give some visual clues about what you want. For example, you can pat your leg or snap your fingers. As soon as your puppy comes running over to you, offer a reward.

Off

This is not the same as teaching your dog not to jump on people (Chapter 8). This command is specifically to get your dog off furniture or surfaces that may be dangerous. This is training that you will need to be prepared to do on the fly because you are training your dog to stop an action. This means you have to react to that undesirable action. Having treats on hand will be essential when you see your dog getting up on things you don't want him to be on.

1. Wait for your dog to put his paws on something that you don't want him on.

2. Say "Off" and lure him away with a treat that you keep just out of his reach.

3. Say "Yes" and give him a treat as soon as his paws are off the surface.

Repeat this every time you see the behavior. It will likely take at least half a dozen times before your dog understands he should not perform the action anymore. Over time, switch from treats to praise or playing with a toy.

Leave It

This is a difficult training command, but you need to teach your dog leave it for when you are out on a walk and want him to ignore other people or dogs.

1. Let your dog see that you have treats in your hand, then close it. Your fist should be close enough for your dog to sniff the treat.

2. Say "Leave it" when your dog starts to sniff your hand.

3. Say "Yes" and give your dog a treat when he turns his head away from the treats. Initially, this will probably take a while as your dog will want those treats. Don't continue to say "Leave it" as your dog should not be learning that you will give a command more than once. You want him to learn that he must do what you say the first time you say it, which is why treats are recommended in the beginning. If a minute or more passes after giving the command, you can then issue it again, but make sure your canine is focused on you and not distracted.

These sessions should only last about five minutes and it will take your dog some time to learn, as you are teaching him to ignore something he does naturally. When he starts to understand and looks away when you say leave it without spending much time sniffing, you can move on to more advanced versions of the training.

1. Leave your hand open so that your dog can see the treats.

2. Say "Leave it" when your dog starts to show interest (this will probably be almost immediately, especially since you won't have your hand closed, so be prepared).

   a. Close your fist if your dog continues to sniff or gets near the treats in your hand.

   b. Give your dog a treat from your other hand if he stops.

Repeat these steps until your dog finally stops trying to sniff the treats. When your dog seems to have this down, move on to the most difficult version of this command.

1. Place treats on the ground, or let your dog see you hide them, and stay close to those treats.

2. Say "Leave it" when your dog starts to show interest in sniffing the treats.

   a. Place a hand over the treats if he doesn't listen.

   b. Give a treat if your dog does listen.

From here, you can start training while standing further from the treat with your dog leashed so you can stop him if needed. Then start to use other things that your dog loves, such as a favorite toy or another tempting treat that you don't usually give him.

Drop It

This is going to be one of the most difficult commands you will teach your puppy because it goes against both your puppy's instincts and interests. Your puppy wants to keep whatever he has, so you are going to have to offer him something better instead. It is essential to teach the command early though, as your Shar-Pei could be very destructive in the early days. Furthermore, this command could save your pooch's life. He is likely to lunge at things that look like food when you are out for a walk and this command will get him to drop anything potentially hazardous that he picks up.

Start with a toy and a treat, or a large treat that your dog cannot eat in a matter of seconds, such as a rawhide. Make sure the treat you have is one that your puppy does not get very often so that there is motivation to drop the toy or big treat.

1. Give your puppy the toy or large treat. If you want to use a clicker too, pair it with the exciting treat that you will use to help convince your puppy to drop the treat.

2. Show your puppy the exciting treat.

3. Say "Drop it" and when he drops the treat or toy, tell him good and hand over the exciting treat while picking up the item.

4. Repeat this immediately after your puppy finishes eating the exciting treat.

You will need to keep reinforcing this command for months after it is learned because it is not a natural instinct. This is one of those rare times when you must use a really irresistible treat because your puppy needs something to convince him to drop a cherished toy, or, more importantly, food that he shouldn't be eating.

Quiet

Shar-Pei are known for being a quiet breed, so you probably won't have much to do with this command. If you find your puppy is already quiet, you don't need to worry about training him not to bark.

If you do have a puppy that does tend to bark, you may want to train the pup not to do it too often. Initially, you can use treats sparingly to reinforce quiet if your pup enjoys making noise.

1. When your puppy barks for no obvious reason, tell him to be quiet and place a treat nearby. It is almost guaranteed that the dog will fall silent to sniff the treat.

2. If your dog does fall silent, say "Good dog" or "good quiet."

It will not take too long for your puppy to understand that quiet means no barking.

If you want your Shar-Pei to be more of a watchdog, you will need to provide some guidance on when he should bark. This is a more advanced type of training, and Shar-Pei all react differently. A professional can help tailor the approach to training your dog when to bark at people at the door. Otherwise, you will want your dog to know that he shouldn't be randomly barking at birds at the window or squirrels running around in the yard.

Where To Go From Here

"The Shar Pei are highly intelligent and easily trained but need boundaries set early. A basic obedience class between 4-5 months of age will reap many benefits as your dog becomes an adult."

Sheila Marquart
Tuck 'N Roll Acres

Shar-Pei are a breed that is fairly easy to train. However, there is a lot of benefit from taking breeds that tend to be aggressive to classes. Your dog will enjoy the extra socialization if you want to take him to a puppy or obedience class. It is a safe environment and a great opportunity for both of you to learn, and there will be an expert present to instruct you in the best way to teach your pup how to act.

For Shar-Pei, you should have all of this training completed between three and six months. Until all of these commands are learned, it is best to avoid other types of advanced training. Between six and twelve months, you should be able to move to tricks, if your dog is willing to do them. Things like fetch and other games may be fun for your Shar-Pei, especially if the pup learns to play when young. Shar-Pei aren't known for being entertainers (at least not intentionally), and with their independent nature, they may not always be interested in tricks for fun, but they will love things that include interacting with their families. It is a good idea to train your Shar-Pei to do some fun activities as they do get bored easily (all intelligent dog breeds do) and yet they are limited in how active they can be because of their short snouts. Since you can't jog with your dog, planning to do more fun activities around your home can help you keep your Shar-Pei in shape and entertained.

Puppy Classes

Puppies can begin to go to puppy school as early as 6 weeks. This is the beginning of obedience training, but you will need to be careful about interactions with other dogs until your puppy has completed his vaccinations. Talk with your vet about when is a good time to begin classes, or at least a safe time. Your vet may be able to recommend good puppy training classes in your area.

Photo Courtesy of Hayley Sellars

The primary purpose of these classes is socialization. Studies have shown that a third of puppies have minimal exposure to new people and dogs during the first 20 weeks of their life, which can make the outside world scarier. The puppy classes give you and your puppy a chance to learn how to meet and greet other people and dogs in a strictly controlled environment. Dogs that attend these classes are much friendlier and are less stressed about things like large trucks, loud noises, and visitors. They are also less likely to be nervous or suffer from separation anxiety.

It is also good training for you. In the same studies, people who attended these classes were better able to react appropriately when a puppy was disobedient or misbehaved. The classes teach you how to train your puppy and how to deal with the emerging headstrong nature of your dog.

Many classes will help you with some of the basic commands, like sit and down. Look for a class that also focuses on socialization so that your puppy can get the most out of the class.

Obedience Training

After your puppy graduates from puppy school and understands most of the basic commands, you can switch to obedience classes. Obedience classes are more difficult, but they shouldn't be that much of a challenge for a Shar-Pei. Some trainers offer at-home obedience training, but it is best to find a class so that your dog can continue socialization. If your puppy attends puppy classes, the trainers can provide you with the next classes that they recommend. Dogs of nearly any age can attend obedience training classes, though your dog should be old enough to listen.

Obedience training usually includes the following:

- Teaching or reinforcing basic commands, like sit, stay, come, and down.

- How to walk without pulling on the leash.

- How to properly greet people and dogs, including not jumping on them.

Obedience school is as much about training you as training your dog. It helps you learn how to train while getting your dog through basic commands and how to behave for basic tasks, like greetings and walking. Classes usually last between 7 and 10 weeks.

Ask your vet for recommendations. If your vet doesn't have any recommendations, take time to thoroughly research your options. Look at the following details when evaluating trainers:

- Are they certified, particularly the CPDT-KA certification?

- How many years have they been training dogs?

- Do they have experience with training Shar-Pei?

- Can you participate in the training? If the answer is no, do not use that trainer. You have to be a part of your dog's training because the trainer won't be around for most of your dog's life. Therefore, your dog has to learn to listen to you.

Obedience training does not help with serious behavioral issues. If your dog has anxiety, depression, or other serious behavioral problems, you need to hire a trainer to help your dog work through those issues. Do your research to make sure your selected trainer is an expert, preferably with experience with intelligent, strong-willed dogs. If possible, find someone who has experience dealing with Shar-Pei.

Once your Shar-Pei has the basic commands down and has done well in obedience training, you can start to do other more enjoyable training. As long as your Shar-Pei did well in the classes, you should not need a trainer because your dog will listen to you. By this point, you should be able to tell if your dog is interested, and you will definitely have more of an idea if you want to pursue more difficult training given your dog's personality.

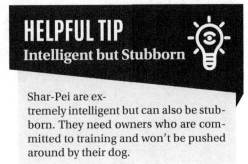

HELPFUL TIP
Intelligent but Stubborn

Shar-Pei are extremely intelligent but can also be stubborn. They need owners who are committed to training and won't be pushed around by their dog.

CHAPTER 12
Nutrition

"You must feed your Shar-Pei a good, high quality food. Doing so will save you many trips to the vet for problems. It does not have to be organic or raw, but read the label to ensure it has high-quality ingredients. Puppies should be fed adult dog food from the beginning with a low protein content. They mature more quickly than some breeds and therefore growth plates grow faster. Puppy food is too rich for them to be on."

Kathleen Probst
Conrad Knoll Chinese Shar-Pei

Photo Courtesy
of Nicola Coltelli

Shar-Pei aren't known for being bottomless pits, but that doesn't mean they don't enjoy food. You will need to be careful to ensure that your Shar-Pei remains at a healthy weight through moderate exercise. With bloat being another potential issue (covered in more detail in Chapter 16), you want to keep your Shar-Pei happy and healthy.

It is far too easy to give your dog too many treats, especially if everyone in your family "trains" the dog. If everyone becomes accustomed to training the dog with praise or toys instead of treats, then your dog's weight and stomach will be less problematic.

HELPFUL TIP
Food Allergies

Shar-Pei are prone to a wide variety of skin problems, more so than other dog breeds. Food allergies can be one cause of skin issues in dogs. The most common dog food allergies are chicken, beef, wheat, dairy, egg, lamb, soy, pork, fish, and rabbit. If your Shar-Pei has skin issues, find a food that doesn't include any of these common allergens.

Some Shar-Pei also have food allergies, so a grain-free diet is recommended. Keep this in mind if you don't want to read through the whole chapter.

Why A Healthy Diet Is Important

Just because your Shar-Pei is active doesn't mean that he is burning all of the calories he takes in, especially if you have an open treat policy. Just as you should not be eating all day, your puppy shouldn't be either. If you have a very busy schedule, it will be entirely too easy to have substantial lapses in activity levels while you are home. Your Shar-Pei isn't going to understand your schedule changes, just the fact that there is usually a certain amount of food going into his mouth, regardless of his activity level. This means he is likely to gain weight when you keep the calories the same while reducing the activities.

You need to be aware of roughly how many calories your dog eats a day, including treats. Be aware of your dog's weight so you can see when he is putting on pounds. This will key you in to when you should adjust how much food your Shar-Pei eats a day, or change food to something with more nutritional value but fewer calories.

Always talk with your vet if you have concerns about your Shar-Pei's weight.

Dangerous Foods

Dogs can eat raw meat without having to worry about the kinds of problems a person will encounter. However, there are some human foods that could be fatal to your Shar-Pei. You should keep these foods away from all dogs:

- Apple seeds
- Chocolate
- Coffee
- Cooked bones (they can kill a dog when the bones splinter in the dog's mouth or stomach)
- Corn on the cob (the cob is deadly to dogs; corn off the cob is fine)
- Grapes/raisins
- Macadamia nuts
- Onions and chives
- Peaches, persimmons, and plums
- Tobacco (your Shar-Pei will not know that it is not a food and may eat it if it's left out)
- Xylitol (a sugar substitute in candies and baked goods)
- Yeast

Photo Courtesy of Shelby Hoyt

In addition to these potentially deadly foods, the Canine Journal has a lengthy list of other foods (http://www.caninejournal.com/foods-not-to-feed-dog/) that should be avoided.

Canine Nutrition

The dietary needs of a dog are significantly different from a human's needs. People are more omnivorous than dogs, meaning they require a wider range of nutrients to be healthy. Canines are largely carnivorous, and protein is a significant dietary requirement. However, they need more than just protein to be healthy.

The following table provides the primary nutritional requirements for dogs.

Nutrient	Sources	Puppy	Adult
Protein	Meat, eggs, soybeans, corn, wheat, peanut butter	22.0% of diet	18.0% of diet
Fats	Fish oil, flaxseed oil, canola oil, pork fat, poultry fat, safflower oil, sunflower oil, soybean oil	8.0 to 15.0% of diet	5.0 to 15.0% of diet
Calcium	Dairy, animal organ tissue, meats, legumes (typically beans)	1.0% of diet	0.6% of diet
Phosphorus	Meat and pet supplements	0.8% of diet	0.5% of diet
Sodium	Meat, eggs	0.3% of diet	0.06% of diet

The following are the remaining nutrients dogs require, all of them less than 1% of a puppy's or adult's diet:

- Arginine
- Histidine
- Isoleucine
- Leucine
- Lysine
- Methionine + cystine
- Phenylalanine + tyrosine
- Threonine
- Tryptophan
- Valine
- Chloride

It is best to avoid giving your dog human foods with a lot of sodium and preservatives.

Water is also absolutely essential to keeping your dog healthy. There should always be water in your dog's water bowl, so make a habit of checking it several times a day so that your dog does not get dehydrated.

Proteins And Amino Acids

Since dogs are carnivores, protein is one of the most important nutrients in a healthy dog's diet (although they should not eat meat nearly as exclusively as their close wolf relatives; dogs' diets and needs have changed significantly since they became companions to humans). Proteins contain the necessary amino acids for your dog to produce glucose, which is essential for giving your dog energy.

A lack of protein in your dog's diet will result in him being lethargic. His coat may start to look dull and he is likely to lose weight. Conversely, if your dog gets too much protein, your dog's body will store the excess protein as fat, meaning he will gain weight.

Meat is typically the best source of protein, and it is recommended since a dog's dietary needs are significantly different from a human's needs. However, it is possible for a dog to have a vegetarian diet as long as you ensure that your dog gets the necessary protein through other sources, and you

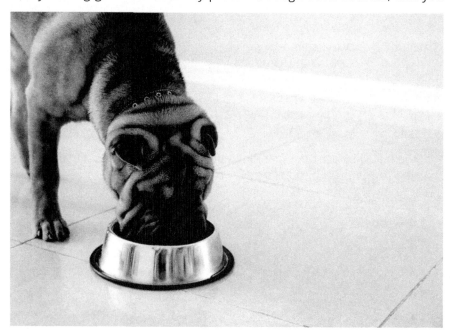

will need to include supplemental vitamin D in his food. If you plan to feed your dog a vegetarian diet, talk to your vet first. It is incredibly difficult to ensure that a carnivore gets adequate protein with a vegetarian diet, especially puppies, so you will need to dedicate a lot of time to research and discussions with nutrition experts to ensure that your dog is getting the necessary proteins for his needs.

Fat And Fatty Acids

Most of the fats that your dog needs also come from meat, though seed oils can provide a lot of the necessary healthy fats too, with peanut butter being one of the most common sources. Fats are broken down into fatty acids, which your dog needs for fat-soluble vitamins that help with regular cell functions. Perhaps the most obvious benefit of fats and fatty acids is in your dog's coat, which will look and feel much healthier when your dog is getting the right nutrients.

There are a number of potential health issues if your dog does not get adequate fats in his daily diet.

- His coat will look less healthy.

- His skin may be dry and itchy.

- His immune system could be compromised, making it easier for your dog to get sick.

- He may have an increased risk of heart disease.

The primary concern if your dog gets too much fat is that he will become obese, leading to additional health problems. For breeds that are predisposed to heart problems, you need to be particularly careful to ensure your dog gets the right amount of fats in his diet. An estimated 18% of Shar-Pei have heart problems.

Carbohydrates And Cooked Foods

Dogs have been living with humans for millennia, so their dietary needs have evolved like our own. They are able to eat foods with carbohydrates to supplement the energy typically provided by proteins and fats. If you cook grains (such as barley, corn, and rice) prior to feeding them to your dog, it will be easier for your dog to digest those complex carbohydrates. This is something to keep in mind when considering what type of food you will feed your dog as you want to get kibble (dry dog food) that uses meat instead of grains; while your dog can digest food with grains (though your dog may be allergic to wheat), he won't get as much of the nutritional value as he would from food that contains real meat.

Photo Courtesy
of Angharad White

Different Dietary Requirements For Different Life Stages

Different stages of a dog's life have different nutritional needs:

- Puppies
- Adults
- Senior dogs

Puppy Food

Dog food manufacturers produce a completely different type of food for puppies for a very good reason – their nutritional needs are much different than their adult counterparts. During roughly the first 12 months of their lives, puppies' bodies are growing. To be healthy, they need more calories and have different nutritional needs to promote that growth. Puppies can have up to four meals a day, just be careful not to overfeed them, particularly as you use treats during training.

Adult Dog Food

The primary difference between puppy food and adult dog food is that puppy food is higher in calories and nutrients that promote growth. Dog food manufacturers reduce these nutrients in food made for adult dogs as they no longer need to sustain growth. As a general rule, when a dog reaches about 90% of his predicted adult size, you should switch to adult dog food.

The size of your dog is key in determining how much to feed him. The following table is a general recommendation on how much to feed your adult Shar-Pei a day. Initially, you may want to focus on the calories as you try to find the right balance for your dog.

Dog Size	Calories
50 lbs.	1,350 during hot months
	2,000 during cold months
70 lbs.	1,680 during hot months
	2,500 during cold months

143

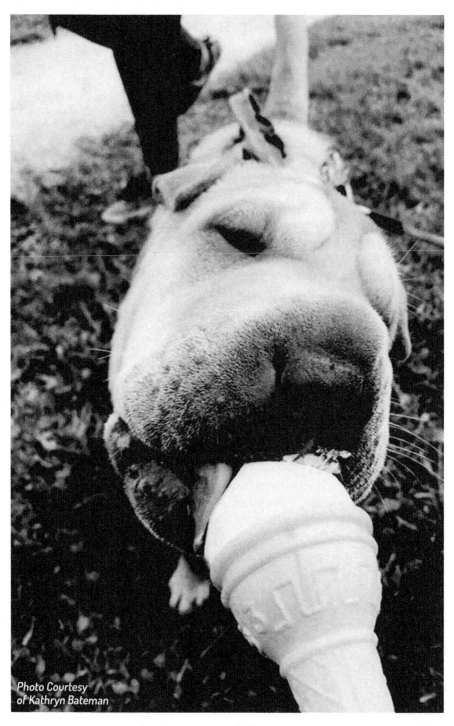

Photo Courtesy
of Kathryn Bateman

It is recommended to feed Shar-Pei twice a day, so you can divide up the calories according to that schedule. Keep in mind that these recommendations are per day, and not per meal.

If you plan to add wet food, pay attention to the total calorie intake and adjust how much you feed your dog between the kibble and wet food. In other words, the total calories in the kibble and wet food should balance out so as not to exceed your dog's needs. The same is true if you give your dog a lot of treats over the course of the day. You should factor treat calorie counts into how much you feed your dog at mealtimes.

If you plan to feed your dog homemade food, you will need to learn more about nutrition, and you will need to pay close attention to calories, and not cup measurements.

Senior Dog Food

Senior dogs aren't always capable of being as active as they were in their younger days. If you notice your dog slowing down or see that your dog isn't able to take longer walks because of joint pain or a lack of stamina, that is a good sign that your dog is entering his senior years. Consult with your vet when you think it is time to change the type of food you give your dog.

The primary difference between adult and senior dog food is that senior dog food has less fat and more antioxidants to help fight weight gain. Senior dogs also need more protein, which will probably make your dog happy because that usually means more meat and meat flavors. Protein helps to maintain your dog's aging muscles. He should be eating less phosphorous during his golden years to avoid the risk of developing hyperphosphatemia. This is a condition where dogs have excessive amounts of phosphorous in their bloodstream, and older dogs are at greater risk of developing it. Phosphorous is largely found in bones to help with muscle contractions and the nerves. The level of phosphorous in the body is controlled by the kidneys. As such, elevated levels of phosphorous are usually an indication of a problem with the kidneys.

Senior dog food has the right number of calories for the reduced activity, so you shouldn't need to adjust how much food you give your dog, unless you notice that he is putting on weight. Consult your vet before you adjust the amount of food or if you notice that your dog is putting on weight. This could be a sign of a senior dog ailment.

Your Dog's Meal Options

You have three primary choices for what to feed your dog, or you can use a combination of the three, depending on your situation and your dog's specific needs:

- Commercial food
- Raw diet
- Homemade diet

Commercial Food

Make sure that you are buying the best dog food that you can afford. Take the time to research each of your options, particularly the nutritional value of the food, and make this an annual task. You want to make sure that the food you are giving your dog is high quality. Always account for your dog's size, energy levels, and age. Your puppy may not need puppy food for as long as other breeds and dog food for seniors may not be the best option for your own senior Shar-Pei.

Pawster provides several great articles about which commercial dog foods are good for Shar-Pei. Since new foods frequently come on the market, check back occasionally to see if there are newer, better foods available.

If you aren't sure about which brand of food is best, talk with the breeder about what foods they recommend. Breeders are really the best guides for you here, as they are experts, but you can ask your vet too.

Some dogs may be picky, and they can certainly get tired of having the same food repeatedly. Just as you switch up your meals, you can change what your Shar-Pei eats. While you shouldn't frequently change the brand of food, you can get foods that have different flavors. You can also change the taste by adding a bit of wet (canned) food. This is an easy change to make, giving your dog a different canned food (usually just about 1/4 to 1/3 of the can for a meal, depending on your dog's size) with each meal.

For more details on commercial options, check out Dog Food Advisor. They provide reviews on the different brands, as well as providing information on recalls and contamination issues.

Commercial Dry Food

Dry dog food often comes in bags, and it is what the vast majority of people feed their dogs.

Dry Dog Food

PROS	CONS
• Convenience	• Requires research to ensure you don't buy doggie junk food
• Variety	
• Availability	• Packaging is not always honest
• Affordability	• Recalls for food contamination
• Manufacturers follow nutritional recommendations (not all of them follow this, so do your brand research before you buy)	• Loose FDA nutritional regulations
	• Low quality food may have questionable ingredients
• Specially formulated for different canine life stages	
• Can be used for training	
• Easy to store	

The convenience and ease on your budget means that you are almost certainly going to buy kibble for your dog. This is perfectly fine, and most dogs will be more than happy to eat kibble. Just know what brand you are currently feeding your dog, and pay attention to kibble recalls to ensure you stop feeding your dog a particular food if necessary. Check out the following sites regularly to make sure your dog's food has not been recalled:

- Dog Food Recalls – Dog Food Advisor
- American Kennel Club
- Dog Food Guide

Commercial Wet Food

Most dogs prefer wet dog food to kibble, but it is also more expensive. Wet dog food can be purchased in larger packs that can be very easy to store.

Wet Dog Food

PROS	CONS
• Helps keep dogs hydrated • Has a richer scent and flavor • Easier to eat for dogs with dental problems (particularly those missing teeth) or if a dog has been ill • Convenient and easy to serve • Unopened, it can last between 1 and 3 years • Balanced based on current pet nutrition recommendations	• Dog bowls must be washed after every meal • Can soften bowel movements • Can be messier than kibble • Once opened, it has a very short shelf life, and should be covered and refrigerated • More expensive than dry dog food, and comes in small quantities • Packaging is not always honest • Recalls for food contamination • Loose FDA regulations

Like dry dog food, wet dog food is convenient, and picky dogs are much more likely to eat it than kibble. When your dog gets sick, use wet dog food to ensure that he is still eating and gets the necessary nutrition each day. It may be a bit harder to switch back to kibble once your Shar-Pei is healthy, but you can always continue to add a little wet food to make each meal more appetizing.

Raw Diet

For dogs like Shar-Pei that have food allergies, raw diets can help prevent an allergic reaction to wheat and processed foods. Raw diets are heavy in raw meats, bones, vegetables, and specific supplements. Some of the benefits to a raw diet include:

- Improves your dog's coat and skin
- Improves immune system
- Improves health (as a result of better digestion)
- Increases energy
- Increases muscle mass

Raw diets are meant to give your dog the kind of food he ate before being domesticated. It means giving your dog uncooked meats, whole (uncooked) bones, and a bit of dairy products. It doesn't include any processed food of any kind – not even food cooked in your kitchen.

There are potential risks to this diet. Dogs have been domesticated for millennia, and their digestive system has evolved as they have. Trying to force them back on the kind of diet they used to eat does not always work as intended because they may not be able to fully digest it anymore. There are also a lot of risks with feeding dogs uncooked meals, particularly if the food has been contaminated. Things like bacteria pose a serious risk and can be transferred to you if your dog gets sick. Many medical professionals also warn about the dangers of giving dogs bones, even if they are uncooked. Bones can splinter in your dog's mouth, puncturing the esophagus or stomach.

The Canine Journal provides a lot of information about the raw diet, including how to transition your current dog to this diet and different recipes for your dog.

Homemade Diet

If you regularly make your own food (from scratch, not with a microwave or boxed meal), it really doesn't take that much more time to provide an equally healthy meal for your companion.

Keeping in mind the foods that your Shar-Pei absolutely should not eat, you can mix some of the food you make for yourself into your Shar-Pei's meal. Just make sure to add a bit more of what your Shar-Pei needs into the food bowl. Although you and your Shar-Pei have distinctly different dietary needs, you can tailor your foods to include nutrients that your dog needs.

Do not feed your Shar-Pei from your plate. Split the food, placing your dog's meal into a bowl so that your canine understands that your food is just for you. The best home-cooked meals should be planned in advance so that your Shar-Pei is getting the right nutritional balance.

Typically, 50% of your dog's food should be animal protein (fish, poultry, and organ meats). About 25% should be full of complex carbohydrates. The remaining 25% should be from fruits and vegetables, particularly foods like pumpkin, apples, bananas, and green beans. These foods provide additional flavor that your Shar-Pei will probably love while making him feel full faster, so that the chance of overeating is reduced.

The following are a few sites you can use to learn to make meals for canines. Some of them are not Shar-Pei specific, so if you have more than one dog, these meals can be made for all of your furry canine friends:

- iPupster
- DORG Daily Diet
- Dogsaholic

Scheduling Meals

Your Shar-Pei will likely expect you to stick to a schedule, and that definitely includes mealtimes. If treats and snacks are something you establish as normal early on, your dog will believe that treats are also a part of the routine.

For puppies, plan to have three or four meals, while adults and seniors should typically have two meals a day.

Food Allergies And Intolerance

"Shar-pei do not tolerate soy well, so a soy free food is best. There have been many debates within the breed regarding the best diet for Shar-pei. I've found as long as you feed a quality adult food low in protein and fat, they generally do well. However, dietary are often dog specific, so it will ultimately depend upon how your dog handles a specific food."

Debbie Raynor
DC Shar-pei

Whenever you start your dog on a new type of dog food (even if it is the same brand that your dog is accustomed to, but a different flavor), you need to monitor him as he becomes accustomed to it. Food allergies are fairly common in Shar-Pei, so you will need to be aware of the symptoms. Food allergies in dogs tend to manifest themselves as hot spots, which are similar to rashes in humans. Your dog may start scratching or chewing specific spots on his body. His fur could start falling out around those spots.

Some dogs don't have a single hot spot, but the allergy shows up on their entire coat. If your Shar-Pei seems to be shedding more fur than normal, take him to the vet to be checked for food allergies.

If you do give your dog something that his stomach cannot handle, it will probably be obvious when your dog is unable to hold his bowels. If he is already housetrained, he will probably either pant at you or whimper to let you know that he needs to go outside. Get him outside as quickly as you can so that he does not have an accident. Flatulence will also probably occur more often if your Shar-Pei has a food intolerance.

Since the symptoms of food allergies and tolerances can be similar to a dog's reaction to nutritional deficiencies (particularly a lack of fats in a dog's diet), you should visit your vet if you notice any problems with your dog's coat or skin.

Slobbering And Drooling

One thing to know about a Shar-Pei's eating and drinking is that they aren't exactly the cleanest at doing either one. There will be a lot of drool, and it will feel like nearly as much water is around the bowl as in your dog's belly after he's had a drink. Those jaws are adorable – as are the wrinkles – but they also present a problem when drinking and eating. It's not a big problem, and you will adore your Shar-Pei despite the regular mess he makes. Just be aware and plan to have a towel under the food and water dishes. You will need to change the towel regularly as it will get very wet over the course of the day.

CHAPTER 13
Loving And Loyal, Your Pup Will Love To Play If You Do It Right

Shar-Pei are incredibly loyal and loving dogs, and they make fantastic companions. The fact that they are protective of their people just makes you want to let them know how much you appreciate everything they do for you. The fact that they can be so enthusiastic about spending time with their pack can make play time that much more enjoyable. While you do need to ensure your dog gets adequate exercise, you also have to make sure he doesn't overheat. During hot days, entertain him as best you can inside and walk him during the mornings and evenings when it is cooler.

Though Shar-Pei aren't known for being particularly playful, they can be if you join them. Watching those blue-black tongues hanging out in anticipation of having fun can really make you feel fantastic.

This chapter covers the many different games and activities you and your Shar-Pei can enjoy to best play to his strengths and natural abilities.

Photo Courtesy of Alyson Dean

Photo Courtesy
of Jessica Donohue

Exercise Needs

"The Shar-Pei do not need a lot of exercise. they are happy and very content with a brisk walk around the block, or a romp in the backyard. The breed is not well suited for 5 mile hikes up a mountain or a bike ride run. They prefer the couch to the track."

Sheila Marquart
Tuck 'N Roll Acres

Shar-Pei are one of the few breeds that tend to adapt their energy levels to their people. If you like to be active, your pup will enjoy romping outside (though not jogging) or hiking. If you prefer a more sedentary approach to life, just make sure your dog gets adequate exercise through walking or playing in the backyard. Some Shar-Pei will enjoy learning tricks, but not all of them like to be told what to do in the name of fun. Having a few activities that you can do together will be a lot more enjoyable for both you and your Shar-Pei than tricks.

As with any intelligent breed, you do need to make sure that there is enough regular mental engagement to ensure that your dog doesn't get bored. A bored Shar-Pei can be a destructive one, and no amount of training will stop that. Part of adopting an intelligent breed is accepting that you are going to need to ensure your dog is happily occupied. Fortunately, that should be fairly easy because Shar-Pei love to spend time with their people. Just like you play games with your kid, it is very easy to play games with your Shar-Pei.

A Wide, Easy Activity Range

Initially, it may seem difficult to entertain a Shar-Pei, but that's really only because people tend to think that all dogs have a certain way to play. Once you get used to the idea of playing a bit differently, you'll see just how easy it is to keep a Shar-Pei happily entertained.

Tracking

With their history as working dogs, there is a lot you can do with your Shar-Pei that plays to their nature. One of the best and most entertaining activities is tracking. Put your adorable pup to work doing something fun for both of you.

This game starts with treats, and your Shar-Pei is going to follow his nose to find them. They have an amazing sense of smell, so over time you can get increasingly more creative in how you hide those treats. When your dog is a puppy, you can hide the goodies in fairly obvious places. Then as he starts to understand the game, you can start making the treat hiding spots a little trickier. Just make sure to know roughly how many calories you're giving your dog at a time. You want to make sure you aren't overfeeding your Shar-Pei.

You can also use your Shar-Pei's favorite toy with some scent added to it. This will let you play for as long as you want without having to worry about your dog getting too many calories. The scent can be added by rubbing some form of meat on the toy (preferably a toy that is rubber, and not a stuffed animal) or by hiding a small treat in the toy. There are some toys that have special pouches for treats, but you won't need to always add the treat since the toy probably already smells like treats.

FUN FACT
"Bone Mouth" Vs. "Meat Mouth"

Shar-Pei come in two different muzzle types. "Bone mouth" Shar-Pei have narrower muzzles, while "meat mouth" Shar-Pei have wider, fleshier muzzles. While the meat mouth look is more popular, the extra padding in the muzzle can contribute to slobbering, snoring, breathing problems, and poor tooth alignment.

More Obedience – For Fun!

Beyond basic commands and obedience classes, you can make a game of obedience. Given how headstrong Shar-Pei can be, the reminders can be very beneficial. Since it feels more like a game, it's a great way to reinforce the kind of behavior you want your dog to have.

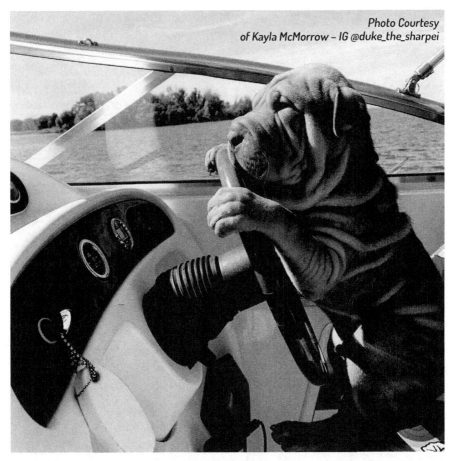

*Photo Courtesy
of Kayla McMorrow – IG @duke_the_sharpei*

This can be as simple as going over the three most important commands for your dog to know for his own safety: sit, stay, and come. A regular review of these with treats will be welcome to your pup because it's always nice to get a reward. Using praise will be just as welcome because your dog will love to have positive reinforcement from his people.

Beyond the basics, there are a few other commands that could be entertaining. There is always Give kisses if you are all right with a good bit of slobber with your kisses. Dogs love to be able to get up close to their people's faces, so your pup will probably pick up this command faster than any other. Back up is a command that has a lot of potential for fun, and the Shar-Pei is a dog that can learn it without you wanting to rip your hair out. From a practical standpoint you can use it to help you get a bit of space if your dog is overcrowding you (which is possible considering your dog will probably follow you to the kitchen) or to get your dog away from the door so people can enter. Shake is a great command that intelligent dogs do well, and given the wise old look of the breed, shaking is adorable. From Shake, you can move into Wave. This command is nice for saying hello and goodbye.

Other Outdoor Games

Shar-Pei are fairly sturdy dogs that love being outside on hikes and visiting dog parks. You will need to make sure that your dog is well socialized so that there are not any problems with other dogs you encounter, but your Shar-Pei will love the change in scenery and will greatly appreciate some time outside.

Photo Courtesy of Carly Parker

Joining In Your Fun

"While Shar-pei do not require an intense amount of physical exercise, they do need to spend time outdoors. Most prefer to do so with their owners, so walks or runs are a good way to do so. Our dogs are part of the family and go with us to the lake, beach, mountains, wherever we may go. A highly intelligent breed, Shar-pei thrive on interaction with their owner. It is important to not become complacent and continue educating them through their lives."

Debbie Raynor
DC Shar-pei

Just because there is inclement weather doesn't mean that your dog's energy levels will be any lower, or that boredom won't set in, so you'll need to plan to keep your Shar-Pei's exercise schedule consistent, even when you are stuck inside the house. Of course, if you can put your dog out to play in the snow in a backyard, that will be fantastic as he can tire himself out in his excitement. During rain and heat, you need to find the right activities to tire your canine without going outside for extended periods of time. Here are some alternatives to help expend your Shar-Pei's energy.

1. If you don't want to use a toy for chase, you might be able to get your Shar-Pei to chase a laser pointer. This may or may not work as your Shar-Pei may realize that he can't catch it. If he doesn't seem to mind though, it is a great way to get rid of that energy on rainy or cold days.

2. Hide and seek is a game you can play once your dog knows about proper behavior in the home, whether you have him find you or a favorite toy you've hidden.

3. Puzzle toys are a great way to get your dog to move around without you having to do much. Many games come with treats, though what your Shar-Pei will want is something that will keep his interest. If he enjoys toys, something with a squeak will likely be of more interest.

4. Fetch may be a game that your Shar-Pei finds enjoyable, depending on if he's interested in toys. Some of them love running after little things because they used to hunt.

5. Some Shar-Pei enjoy swimming, and if yours does, you should get him a swimming vest. With their short snouts, you need to make sure your Shar-Pei can always keep that adorable face above water.

CHAPTER 14
Grooming – Productive Bonding

"Shar-pei require little grooming, but do need to be brushed regularly and bathed as needed. A hypoallergenic shampoo is best. Toe nails should be trimmed weekly. Get them used to baths at an early age as some are not fond of water."

Debbie Raynor
DC Shar-pei

HELPFUL TIP
Brushing and Bathing

Brush your Shar-Pei at least once a week with a rubber curry brush to remove loose hair before it sheds all over your house. Unless they have a skin problem requiring baths in a special shampoo, Shar-Pei don't need to be bathed more than a few times per year. The most important thing to keep in mind when washing your Shar-Pei is to make sure he is completely dry afterward, especially the wrinkles. Any dampness left in the wrinkles can cause a yeast infection.

Your Shar-Pei will be incredibly easy to groom, though you will need to take extra care of his wrinkles. He won't require a professional to groom him because he has short hair (although if you have an allergic reaction, you may want to have someone else in your home do the grooming). Shar-Pei, as a rule, love to keep themselves clean, so you won't need to bathe your dog more than a few times a year (unless you take him out where he can get really dirty).

Your friend will also need regular attention to his ears and teeth, but mostly you will be doing the same grooming you do with most dogs. You will need to be careful of ear infections because those cute ears tend to trap dirt and encourage infection.

This chapter provides a baseline for making sure your Shar-Pei's coat, face, and nails are clean and healthy.

Grooming Tools

You don't need too many tools to properly groom your Shar-Pei because his hair is too short to tangle or be a real problem. Still, there are a few tools you need. Make sure you have the following items on hand before your puppy or adult dog arrives:

- A short, rubber-bristled brush will be gentle on skin, or a grooming mitt.
- Shampoo (check Bark Space for the latest recommendations for a breed with potential skin conditions) – use a hypoallergenic shampoo.
- Nail trimmers.
- Toothbrush and toothpaste (check the American Kennel Club for the latest recommendations) – use toothpaste made specifically for dogs.

Coat Management

A Shar-Pei does shed, but it doesn't tend to show as much because he has short hair. In most cases, once a week will be enough times to brush your dog since this will pick up most of the hair. It is also the perfect time to check the folds in the skin to make sure the wrinkles are not infected.

If you have allergies, your Shar-Pei may shed enough to potentially trigger those allergies. The coarse hair has also been known to cause rashes in some people, though this is rare. If you have a reaction, you can get a grooming mitt which will make it easy to brush your Shar-Pei without having to touch his bristly fur as much.

Puppies

Grooming a puppy is fairly universal in how difficult it can be, but a Shar-Pei's coat is fairly easy to manage – even if it is a little difficult to get a puppy to stop squirming. A daily brushing can not only reduce how much your puppy sheds, but it helps you to build a bond with the dog. Yes, it will be a bit challenging in the beginning because puppies don't sit still for long periods of time. There will be a lot of wiggling and attempts to play. Trying to tell your puppy

that the brush is not a toy clearly isn't going to work, so be prepared to be patient during each brushing session.

On the other hand, your pup will be so adorable, you probably won't mind that grooming takes a bit longer. Just make sure you let your pup know that this is a serious effort and playing comes after grooming. Otherwise, your Shar-Pei is going to always try to play, which will make brushing him more time consuming. Plan to brush your puppy after a vigorous exercise session so that your Shar-Pei has far less energy. You can plan to brush once a week to establish a good bond with your puppy. If you find that your puppy has trouble sitting still, you can increase how often you brush the puppy to get him used to it.

Adult Dogs

Brushing your dog once a week is adequate to get rid of the dead and loose fur. Since a Shar-Pei coat is so short, this really is not a time-consuming effort, even if the dog is considered a large dog. Grooming mitts can make it even faster as you can brush a lot of the coat with each stroke. Always look for skin problems, lumps, flea or tick bites, or other problems every time you brush your buddy so that you will know when you need to take him to the vet or just keep an eye on a potential issue.

If you rescued an adult Shar-Pei, it may take a little while to get the dog used to being brushed frequently. If you aren't able to get your dog to feel comfortable with brushing his fur in the beginning, you can work it into your schedule, like training.

Senior Dogs

You can brush your senior dog more often if you would like, as the extra affection and time with you will likely be welcome. After all, he's slowing down, and just relaxing with you will be enjoyable (and the warmth of your hands will feel really good on his aging body). Grooming sessions are a good time to check for issues while giving your older pup a nice massage to ease any pain. While brushing your dog, look for any changes to the skin, such as bumps or fatty lumps. These may need to be mentioned to the vet during a regular visit if the bumps or lumps are very large.

Allergies

If your Shar-Pei is suffering from hot spots or if you notice his coat thinning during grooming sessions, watch for these other problems, which could be a sign of allergies:

- Wounds take longer to heal

- Weak immune system
- Aching joints
- Hair is falling out
- Ear infections

Regular brushing ensures that you are more aware of the state of your Shar-Pei's coat, which can help you more quickly identify when your little dear is suffering from allergies. If you notice these issues, take your Shar-Pei to the vet.

FUN FACT
"Sand Skin"

Literally translated, Shar-Pei means "sand skin," which is a creative way to describe the unique texture of the breed's coat. Many people are allergic to the short, coarse hair of Shar-Pei, so your whole family should spend some time around the breed before bringing one home.

Taking Care Of The Wrinkles

"It is not required to clean their wrinkles or bath them often. They are an extremely clean breed and hate to get dirty. You should however try to wipe their mouth and underchins when eating or drinking to keep the moisture out. I use plain baby wipes. This reduces the chance of pimples or infection growing under there."

Kathleen Probst
Conrad Knoll Chinese Shar-Pei

When you brush your dog's fur once a week, get in the habit of checking the wrinkles in his skin, especially around the face. Yeast and fungus can thrive in these areas if they are not regularly wiped with a lightly damp cloth. If you make this part of the weekly brushing routine, your Shar-Pei will get used to the activity so it won't be as big a deal – the younger your dog is when you can get him accustomed to it, the better.

Bath Time

Your Shar-Pei will only need a bath about once every 6 to 8 weeks, unless he gets really dirty. Avoid washing him too often as it can bother his sensitive skin.

Of course, if your Shar-Pei gets dirty (which may happen whenever you go out exploring or hiking), then you'll need to take the time to bathe your canine after each of these events. Make sure the water isn't too cold or too hot, but comfortably warm. Make sure you don't get his head wet. Washing your dog's face is covered in the next section.

You can use these practices with other kinds of bathing, such as outside or at a public washing facility, modifying them as necessary.

The first few times you bathe your dog, pay attention to the things that bother or scare him. If he is afraid of running water, make sure you don't have the water running when your dog is in the tub. If he moves around a lot when you start to apply the shampoo, it could indicate the smell is too strong. You need to modify the process to make it as comfortable for your dog as possible.

Keep in mind that you have to be patient and calm during the bath. If you get upset or take out your frustration out on your dog, it will make all future baths that much more difficult because your dog will begin to stop trusting you. This isn't a fight for dominance, it is an honest lack of understanding from his standpoint for why you are torturing him when he already does so much to clean himself. Keep a calm, loving tone as you wash your dog to make it a little easier next time. Sure, your Shar-Pei may whine, throw a tantrum, or wiggle excessively, but the better you take it, the more the dog will learn that bathing is simply a part of being in the pack.

Cleaning Eyes And Ears

Shar-Pei have a unique ear structure that increases the odds that they will get ear infections. Regularly checking your dog's ears can help you detect infections early. Look for the following behaviors for signs of a problem:

- Frequent head shaking or tilting
- Regular scratching at ears
- Swollen or red ears
- A smell or discharge from the ears

10

STEPS FOR BATH TIME

1 **GET EVERYTHING YOU WILL NEED IN ONE PLACE**
Make sure you have the following supplies ready: shampoo and conditioner (made for dogs), one large cup, towels, brush, non-slip tub mat.

2 **TAKE YOUR SHAR-PEI OUT FOR A WALK.**
This will both tire your dog and make him a little hotter, which will make the bath less hated – maybe even appreciated.

3 **RUN THE WATER**
Make sure that the temperature is lukewarm but not hot, especially if you have just finished a walk. If you are washing him in a bathtub, you only need enough water to cover up to your pup's stomach.

4 **TALK IN A STRONG CONFIDENT VOICE**
Don't use baby talk. Your Shar-Pei needs a confident leader, not to be treated like an infant.

5 **PLACE THE DOG IN THE TUB**
and use the cup to wash the dog. Don't use too much soap – it isn't necessary. You can fully soak the dog starting at the neck and going to the rump. It is fine to get him wet all at once, then to suds him up, or you can do it a bit at a time if your dog is very wiggly. Just make sure that you don't get any water on his head.

6 **TALK TO YOUR DOG**
while you are bathing him, keeping in mind you need to talk with confidence, not a high tone.

7 **MAKE SURE YOU DON'T GET WATER IN YOUR DOG'S EYES OR EARS**
You don't need to get water on the top of your dog's head. Use a wet hand and gently scrub around his eyes and ears, being careful to avoid getting soap or water in either. Follow the steps in the next section to properly – and carefully – wash your dog's face and very long ears.

8 **RINSE OFF AGAINST THE GRAIN**
Make sure rinse the water up against the natural lay of the fur so that there isn't any shampoo left beneath the hairs.

9 **TOWEL DRY AND BRUSH**
Toweling drying and rushing are great bonding times, towel dry and then brush gently so your Shar-Pei enjoys the process and is excited for the next bath!

10 **GIVE HIM A TREAT**
If he was particularly upset about the bath.

Photo Courtesy
of JJ Aldret

If you notice any problems with your Shar-Pei's ears, make an appointment with your vet. Never try to treat an infection on your own; hydrogen peroxide, cotton swabs, and other cleaning tools should never be used in a dog's ears. Never put anything in your dog's ears. Your vet can help you learn how to clean your dog's ears correctly if infections become common.

Use a washcloth to wash your dog's face and ears. When you bathe your Shar-Pei, be careful not to get water in his ears. You should also make a habit of checking his ears once a week.

Shar-Pei have several genetic eye and ear conditions (Chapter 16), so take the time to always check your dog's eyes while you are grooming him. Cataracts are a fairly common problem for all dogs as they age. If you see cloudy eyes, have your Shar-Pei checked. If he's developing cataracts, you may need to take the pup in to have them removed because cataracts can lead to blindness.

Trimming Nails

"Most Shar-Pei hate to have their feet touched. Cutting nails can be a challenge. Have your vet show you how to clip their nails. Patience, praise and treats for each nail clipped. Don't push your puppy too much. Doing just one nail a day can keep nail clipping from being a bad experience."

Janet Saporito
Thornapple Hill Chinese Shar-Pei

Cutting a Shar-Pei's nails can be difficult because he may not want to allow you to touch his paws. It's best to have an expert cut your dog's nails until you can see how it's done. If you have not cut a dog's nails before, ask a professional like a groomer or vet to teach you since the nails can bleed a lot if done 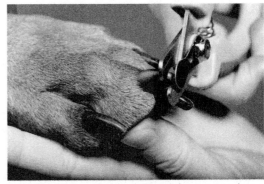 incorrectly. If you already know how to trim a dog's nails, make sure to have some styptic powder nearby in case you cut too much nail off.

If you want to trim your dog's nails yourself, there are nail grinders that can help lessen your worry about cutting them to the quick. However, you will need to make sure that you don't grind too much off the nail. Seek help from a professional to make sure you know how to use the grinder, keep your dog calm, and make sure that it is done safely.

To know when your pup needs his nails cut, pay attention when your dog is walking on hard surfaces to make sure his nails aren't clicking. If they are, then you should increase how often you get your dog's nails trimmed. As a general rule, once a month is recommended.

Oral Health And Brushing Your Dog's Teeth

Shar-Pei need their teeth brushed at least weekly to reduce dental problems as they tend to have problems with their teeth and gums. You probably will want to learn to do it yourself over having to visit a shop once a week. It's also nice to know how to brush your dog's teeth if his breath smells bad or he eats something that smells foul.

Again, you have to learn to be patient and keep it from being an all-out fight with your dog. Brushing a dog's teeth is a little weird, and your Shar-Pei may not be terribly happy with someone putting stuff in his mouth. However, once he is accustomed to it, the task will likely only take a few minutes a day.

Always use a toothpaste that is made for dogs. Human toothpaste can be toxic to dogs. The flavor of dog toothpaste will also make it easier to brush your dog's teeth – or at least entertaining as he tries to eat it. To start brushing your pup's teeth:

Once your dog seems all right with having his teeth brushed with your finger, try the same steps with a canine toothbrush. It may be a similar song and dance in the beginning, but it shouldn't take nearly as long for him to accept the toothbrush. It could take a couple of weeks before you can graduate to a toothbrush.

5

STEPS FOR FINGER BRUSHING YOUR SHAR-PEI TEETH

1

GET YOUR SHAR-PEI COMFORTABLE
Put a little toothpaste on your finger and let you SP sniff and lick it. Once they do, praise them for trying something new!

2

POSITION YOUR PUP FOR EASY CONTROL
In an either sitting or kneeling position, Place your SP in between your legs with his head facing away from you. This will allow you to control him as he squirms at first.

3

BRUSH IN SMALL CIRCLES AROUND EACH TOOTH
After reapplying toothpaste to your finger, lift up your dog's upper lip, and begin to rub in circles around your Shar-Pei's teeth. Your pup will likely make it difficult by constantly trying to lick your finger. Give your puppy praise when he doesn't wiggle too much. Try to move in a circular motion around each tooth, this will be hard with the smaller sharper teeth!

4

MASSAGE THE GUMS
Try to massage both the top and bottom gums. It is likely that the first few times you won't be able to do much more than get your finger in your dog's mouth, and that's okay. Over time, your puppy will learn to listen as training elsewhere helps your dog understand when you are giving commands

5

STAY POSITIVE
No, you probably won't be able to clean the puppy's teeth properly for a while, and that is perfectly fine so long as you keep working at it patiently and consistently.

CHAPTER 15
General Health Issues: Allergies, Parasites, And Vaccinations

Because of their tendency to get infections in their wrinkles, you need to be very careful of the environmental factors that your Shar-Pei is exposed to every day. He is going to love going out to new places and hiking in forests – the breed loves doing new things and exploring. You don't want to deny your dog the things he loves; however, you do need to make sure that your excursions don't exacerbate any environmental allergies your dog might have, and you will have to monitor him for parasites. For example, if you live near a wooded area, your dog is at a greater risk of ticks than a dog that lives in the city. Talk to your vet about particular environmental risks.

Photo Courtesy of Renee and Gimy Blandu

The Role Of Your Veterinarian

From getting annual vaccines updated to health checkups, regularly scheduled vet visits will make sure that your Shar-Pei stays healthy. If your Shar-Pei seems sluggish or less excited than usual, it could be a sign that there is something wrong with him. Fortunately, the breed's personality tends to make it easy to tell when a dog isn't feeling well. Annual visits to the vet will ensure there isn't a problem that is slowly draining the energy or health from your dog.

Health checkups also make sure that your Shar-Pei is aging well. If there are any early symptoms of something potentially wrong with your dog over the years (such as arthritis), an early diagnosis will allow you to start making adjustments early. The vet can help you come up with ways to manage pain and problems that come with the aging process and will be able to recommend adjustments to the schedule to accommodate your canine's aging body and diminishing abilities. This will ensure that you can keep having fun together without hurting your dog.

Vets can provide treatments and/or preventive medications for the different parasites and microscopic threats that your dog may encounter when he is outside, during interactions with other dogs, or from exposure to animals outside your home.

Allergies

Shar-Pei are known for having skin allergies, so you will need to monitor your dog for allergic reactions beyond just food. Instead of sneezing, coughing, and runny noses, dog allergies often present as skin irritations. This is easier to spot on a short-haired Shar-Pei than with many other breeds as you will probably see the irritation, and it will definitely be easy to see if your dog has been chewing on one area of his body more often than others.

The scientific name for environmental allergies is atopic dermatitis, but it's more difficult to tell whether the problem is with the environment or the food you're giving your dog. The symptoms tend to be similar in dogs for both types of allergies:

- Itching/scratching, particularly around the face
- Hot spots
- Ear infections

Photo Courtesy
of Courtney Conway

- Skin infections

- Runny eyes and nose (not as common)

Dogs often develop allergies when they are between 1 and 5 years old. Once they develop an allergy, canines don't outgrow the problem. Usually dog allergies are related to skin exposure, but some canines can be allergic to inhaling microscopic particles, such as dust, molds, and pollens.

Since the symptoms are the same for food and environmental allergies, you will need to talk to your vet about determining the cause. If your dog has a food allergy, all you have to do is change the food that you give him. If he has an environmental allergy, he will need medication, just as humans do. Because of this, you will want to know if the problem is from something seasonal (like pollen) or something year round so you will know when to treat your dog.

As with humans, completely eliminating the problem really isn't reasonable – there is only so much you can do to change the environment around your dog. There are several types of medications that can help your dog become less sensitive to the allergens.

- **Antibacterials/Antifungals** – Shampoos, pills, and creams usually do not treat the allergy but address the underlying problems that come with allergies, such as bacterial and yeast infections.

- **Anti-inflammatories** – These are over-the-counter oral medications that are comparable to allergy medicine for people. Don't give your dog any medication without first consulting with the vet. You will need to monitor your dog to see if he has any adverse effects. If your dog has lethargy, diarrhea, or dehydration, consult with your vet.

- **Immunotherapy** – A series of shots can help reduce your dog's sensitivity to whatever he is allergic to. This is something you can do at home after learning how to give the shots from your vet. Scientists are also developing an oral version of the medication to make it easier to take care of your dog.

- **Topical** – This medication tends to be a type of shampoo and conditioner that will remove any allergens from your dog's fur. Giving your dog a warm (not hot) bath can also help relieve itching.

Talk with your vet about the medications that are available for your dog to determine the best treatment for your situation and your Shar-Pei's needs.

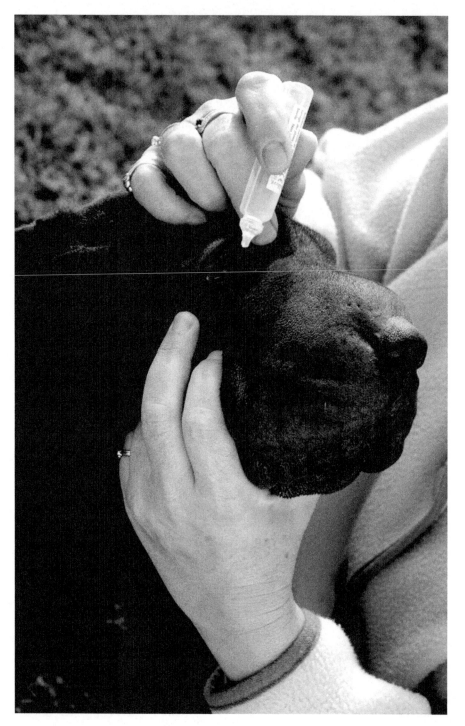

Inhalant And Environmental Allergies

Inhalant allergies are caused by things like dust, pollen, mold, and even dog dander. Your dog might scratch at a particular hot spot or he might paw at his eyes and ears. Some dogs have runny noses and sneeze prolifically, but this is usually in addition to scratching.

Contact Allergies

Contact allergies mean that your dog has touched something that triggers an allergic reaction. Things like wool, chemicals in a flea treatment, and certain grasses can trigger irritation in a dog's skin, even causing discoloration. If left untreated, the allergic reaction can cause the affected area to emit a strong odor and cause fur loss.

Like food allergies, contact allergies are easy to treat because once you know what is irritating your dog's skin, you can remove the problem.

Fleas And Ticks

Shar-Pei tend to love being outside (except when the weather doesn't suit them), so you will need to be very careful about fleas and ticks. Even in your backyard, fleas are a problem nearly year round. Neither parasite is easy to see because of the darker coloring most Shar-Pei tend to have. You can't allow any lapse in flea and tick treatment, even in the winter.

Make it a habit to check for ticks after every outing into the woods, or near long grass or wild plants. Comb through your dog's fur and check his skin for irritation and parasites. Since you will be doing this once a week, you should be able to recognize when there's a change, such as a new bump, for example. Since your dog will be very happy to spend time with you, the skin check shouldn't take long.

Fleas are problematic because they're far more mobile than ticks. The best way to look for fleas is to make it a regular part of your brushing sessions. If you see black specks on the flea comb after brushing through your dog's fur, this could be a sign of fleas. Instead of using a comb, you can also put your dog on a white towel and run your hand over the fur. Fleas and flea dirt are likely to fall on the towel. Fleas often are seen on the stomach, so you may notice them when your pup wants a belly rub. You can also look for behavioral indicators, such as incessant scratching and licking. You will need to use flea preventative products on a regular basis once your puppy reaches an appropriate age.

*Photo Courtesy
of Patricia Buhrman*

Along with being annoying, both can carry parasites and illnesses that can be passed on to you and your dog. Ticks notoriously carry Lyme disease, which can be debilitating or deadly if untreated. Lyme disease symptoms include headaches, fever, and fatigue. The bite itself often has a red circle around it that may grow. Since your dog will likely start to act sluggish after you find a tick attached to his skin, make sure to look for the circular rash, and if you see one or aren't sure, go to the vet to have it checked.

If the tick hasn't latched on, you can just remove it – it hasn't yet bitten your dog. Ticks will fall off your dog once they are full, so if you find a tick on your dog, it will either be looking for a place to latch onto your dog or it will be feeding. Use the following steps to remove the tick if it has latched onto your dog.

1. Apply rubbing alcohol to the area where the tick is.

2. Use tweezers to pull the tick off your dog. Do not use your fingers because infections are transmitted through blood, and you don't want the tick to latch onto you.

3. Examine the spot where the tick was to make sure it is fully removed. Sometimes the head will remain, so you will need to make sure all of the tick is gone.

4. Set up a meeting with the vet to have it checked.

The FDA has issued a warning about some store-bought treatments. Whether you look into purchasing treatments that have to be applied monthly or a collar for constant protection, you need to check the treatment to see if it contains isoxazoline (included in Bravecto, Nexgard, Credelio, and Simparica) because this ingredient can have an adverse effect on some pets. While other ingredients are safe for pets when used in the proper doses, if you use a product that is meant for a larger dog, it can be toxic to your dog. Consult with your vet about recommended treatments to ensure that you get the right dose of flea and tick repellant for your dog's size and needs. When you start applying the treatment, monitor your dog for the following issues:

- Diarrhea/vomiting

- Trembling

- Lethargy

- Seizures

Take your dog to the vet if you notice any of these issues.

Never use any product designed for a dog on a cat or vice versa. If your dog is sick, pregnant, or nursing, you may need to look for an alternative treatment. Flea collars are generally not recommended because they are known to cause problems in pets and people. If you have a cat or young children, you should choose one of the other options for keeping fleas and ticks away. This is because flea collars contain an ingredient that is lethal to felines and which might be carcinogenic to humans.

When you purchase a flea treatment, make sure to read the packaging to find out when is the right time to begin treating your dog based on his current age and size. Different brands have different recommendations, and you don't want to start treating your puppy too early. There are also very important steps to apply the treatment. Make sure you understand all of the steps before you purchase the flea treatment.

If you want to use natural products instead of chemical ones, set aside a few hours to research the alternatives and find out what works best for your Shar-Pei. Verify that any natural products work before you buy them and make sure you consult with your vet. Establishing a regular schedule and adding it to the calendar will help you remember to consistently treat your dog for fleas and ticks each month.

Parasitic Worms

FUN FACT
Small Ears

The small ears of Shar-Pei gave the dogs an advantage during fights, providing less for an opponent to hold onto. However, those small ears are prone to chronic yeast infections thanks to the tiny ear canals not getting proper airflow. Make sure to clean out your Shar-Pei's ears at least once a week.

Although worms are a less common problem than fleas and ticks, they can be far more dangerous. There are a number of types of worms that you should be aware of:

- Heartworms
- Hookworms
- Roundworms
- Tapeworms
- Whipworms

Unfortunately, there isn't an easy-to-recognize set of symptoms to help identify when your dog has worms. However, you can keep an eye out for these symptoms, and if your dog shows them, schedule a visit to the vet.

- Your Shar-Pei is unexpectedly lethargic for at least a few days.

- Patches of fur begin to fall out (this will be noticeable if you brush your Shar-Pei regularly) or if you notice patchy spaces in your dog's coat.

- Your dog's stomach becomes distended (expands) and looks like a potbelly.

- Your Shar-Pei begins coughing, vomiting, has diarrhea, or has a loss in appetite.

If you aren't sure about any symptom, it's always best to get to the vet as soon as possible.

Heartworms

Heartworms are a significant threat to your dog's health and can be deadly as they can both slow and stop blood flow. As such, you should consistently treat your dog with heartworm protection.

Fortunately, heartworms are among the easiest health problems to prevent. There are medications that can ensure your Shar-Pei does not get heartworms. To prevent this very serious problem, you can give your dog a chewable medication, topical medicine, or you can request shots.

This particular parasite is carried by mosquitoes, which are nearly impossible to avoid in most regions of the country. Since heartworms are potentially deadly, taking preventative measures is essential.

If a dog has heartworms, the condition is costly and time-consuming to treat and cure, but it will be well worth all of the work to keep your pup healthy and happy.

1. The vet will draw blood to conduct tests, which can cost as much as $1,000.

2. Treatment will begin with some initial medications, including antibiotics and anti-inflammatory drugs.

3. Following a month of the initial medication, your vet will give your dog three shots over the course of two months.

From the time when the vet confirms that your dog has heartworms until he or she says your dog is clear of the parasite, you will need to be careful when your dog exercises because the worms are in your dog's heart, inhibiting blood flow. Therefore, getting your dog's heart pumping too much can kill him. Considering your Shar-Pei is likely to be energetic, this is going to be a very rough time for both you and your dog. Your vet will tell you how best to exercise your canine during this time.

Treatment will continue after the shots are complete. After about 6 months, your vet will conduct another blood test to ensure that the worms are gone.

Once your dog is cleared of the parasites, you will need to be vigilant about medicating your dog against heartworms. You want to make sure that your poor little guy doesn't suffer through that again. There will be lasting damage to your dog's heart, so you will need to ensure that your dog does not over-exercise.

Intestinal Worms: Hookworms, Roundworms, Tapeworms, And Whipworms

All four of these worms thrive in your dog's intestinal tract, and they get there when your dog eats something contaminated with them. The following are the most common ways that dogs ingest worms:

- Feces
- Small hosts, such as fleas, cockroaches, earthworks, and rodents
- Soil, including licking it from their fur and paws
- Contaminated water
- Mother's milk (if the mother has worms, she can pass it to young puppies when they nurse)

The following are the most common symptoms and problems caused by intestinal parasites:

- Anemia
- Blood loss
- Coughing
- Dehydration
- Diarrhea
- Large intestine inflammation
- Weight loss

If a dog lies in soil with hookworm larvae, the parasite can burrow through the canine's skin. Vets will conduct a diagnostic test to determine if your dog has this parasite. If your dog does have hookworms, your vet will prescribe a de-wormer. You should visit a doctor yourself because humans can get hookworms, too.

Roundworms are kind of like fleas in that they are very common, and at some point in their lives, most dogs have to be treated for them. They primarily eat the digested food in your dog's stomach, getting the nutrients that your dog needs. It is possible for larvae to remain in your dog even after all of the adult worms have been eradicated. Mothers can pass these larvae to their puppies. This means if you have a pregnant Shar-Pei, you will need to have her puppies periodically checked to make sure the inactive larvae aren't passed on to the puppies. The mother will also need to go through the same testing to make sure the worms don't make her sick. In addition to the symptoms listed above, your Shar-Pei may appear to have a potbelly. You may also see the worms in your dog's excrement or vomit.

Photo Courtesy of Vannity Monroid

Tapeworms are usually eaten when they are eggs, usually carried by fleas or from the feces of other animals that have tapeworms. They develop in the canine's small intestine until they are adults. Over time, parts of the tapeworm will break off and become obvious in your dog's waste, which needs to be carefully cleaned up to keep other animals from getting tapeworms. While tapeworms typically aren't fatal, they can cause weight loss while giving your dog a potbelly (depending on how big the worms grow to be in your dog's intestines).

Your vet can test your dog to see if he has tapeworms, and will prescribe a medication, including chewables, tablets, or a medication you can sprinkle on your dog's food. There is a low risk of humans getting tapeworms, with kids being at the greatest risk because of the likelihood that they will play in areas where there is dog waste and then not wash their hands carefully enough afterward. It is possible to contract tapeworms if a person swallows a flea, which is possible if your dog and home have a serious infestation.

Whipworms grow in the large intestine, and in large numbers they can be fatal. Their name is indicative of their appearance, with their tails appearing thinner than the upper section. Like the other worms, you will need to have your dog tested to determine if he is sick.

Keeping up with flea treatments, making sure people pick up behind their pets, and watching to make sure your Shar-Pei doesn't eat trash or animal waste are the best preventative measures to keep your dog safe from getting these parasites.

If your dog has hookworms or roundworms, these can be spread to you from your dog through skin contact. Being treated at the same time as your Shar-Pei can help stop the vicious cycle of continually switching which of you has worms.

Preventative measures against all of these worms can be included with the preventative medication for heartworms. Talk to your vet about the different options to keep your pet from suffering any of these health problems.

Vaccinating Your Shar-Pei

Vaccination schedules are almost universal for all dog breeds, including Shar-Pei. The following list can help you ensure your Shar-Pei receives the necessary shots on schedule. Make sure to add this to your calendar. As a reminder, no shots should be administered during your puppy's very first vet visit. Your new dog already has enough stress with all of the changes in his life. If your puppy is due for more shots soon after arriving at your home, that trip should be scheduled separately, once your puppy feels more comfortable in your home. Until your puppy has completed his vaccinations, you should avoid dogs outside of your home, and keep exposure to your other dogs to a minimum.

The following table provides details on which shots should be administered and when.

Timeline	Shot		
6 to 8 weeks	Bordetella Lyme	Leptospira Influenza Virus-H3N8	DHPP – First shot Influenza Virus-H3N2
10 to 12 weeks	Leptospira Lyme	DHPP – Second shot Influenza Virus-H3N8	Rabies Influenza Virus-H3N2
14 to 16 weeks	DHPP – Third shot		
Annually	Leptospira Lyme	Bordetella Influenza Virus-H3N8	Rabies Influenza Virus-H3N2
Every 3 Years	DHPP Booster	Rabies (if opted for longer duration vaccination)	

These shots protect your dog against a range of ailments. Keep in mind that you will need to make shots an annual part of your dog's vet visits so that you can continue to keep your pup safe. If you would like to learn more about the diseases these vaccinations protect your dog from contracting, check out the Canine Journal. They provide details about the ailments and other information that can help you understand why it is so important to keep up with the shots.

Holistic Alternatives

Wanting to keep a dog from a lot of exposure to chemical treatments makes sense, and there are many good reasons why people are moving to more holistic methods. However, doing this requires a lot more research and monitoring to ensure that the methods are working – and, most importantly, do not harm your dog. Unverified holistic medicines can be a waste of money, or, worse, they can even be harmful to your pet.

If you decide to go with holistic medication, talk with your vet about your options. You can also seek out Shar-Pei experts to see what they recommend before you start using any methods you are interested in trying. Read what scientists have said about the medicine you are considering. There is a chance that the more generic products you buy from a store are actually better than some holistic medications sold in specialty stores.

Make sure you are thorough in your research and that you don't take any unnecessary risks with the health of your Shar-Pei. Things like acupuncture are popular, but these treatments don't have the same effects on dogs as they do on humans. With many sites dedicated to taking care of Shar-Pei, you can find some information on what is recommended. It is possible that something like massage therapy can do a lot to help your dog, especially as he ages. You will need to be careful though because of the potential health problems the breed has. Follow the recommendations on the reputable Shar-Pei sites to provide the best, safest care for your dog. There is even a special type of chiropractic therapy for dogs, but you will need to be careful about finding a reputable chiropractor for your pup so that the treatment doesn't do more harm than good.

CHAPTER 16
Genetic Health Concerns Common To The Shar-Pei

"The average lifespan for the breed as a whole now is 10 to 12 years. As Shar-pei age they are more prone to glaucoma, digestive disorders, hip dysplasia and kidney disease. Having a vet that is familiar with the breed is an integral part of being a Shar-pei owner."

Debbie Raynor
DC Shar-pei

NOT-SO-FUN FACTS
Entropion

Entropion is a condition where a dog's eyelids curl in toward the eye, which causes the eyelashes to rub against the cornea. Not only is it extremely painful, but it can lead to blindness. Shar-Pei are highly prone to entropion and often require surgery to fix the condition.

Unfortunately, Shar-Pei are prone to a number of genetic issues because of irresponsible breeders. While good breeders will help to minimize the risks of their puppies having genetic issues, it is possible that there will be some problems despite their efforts. To make sure your Shar-Pei lives a long, healthy life, you'll need to watch for some of these problems.

Breeders should be able to provide health records in addition to any shot records and required tests. Making sure that the parents are healthy increases the likelihood that your puppy will remain healthy over the course of his entire life. However, there is still a chance that your dog will have one of the following problems even if the parents don't, so you will need to keep an eye on your little friend.

Swollen Hock Syndrome

Swollen hock syndrome is a rare disease, but Shar-Pei have been known to get it, and it has even been given the name familial Shar-Pei fever and systemic amyloidosis because it is primarily a problem for the breed. This is a genetic problem, so even if the parents don't have it, the disease could be passed down to the puppies if the parents are carriers – especially if both are carriers.

The disease is caused by the dog's body being unable to break down the protein amyloid, so that it cannot be fully removed from the body. This causes amyloid to accumulate, damaging the liver and kidneys and potentially causing them to fail.

If your dog appears to be unusually lethargic, does not appear to be hungry, and seems to have a high temperature and shivers, this could be the cause. You may be able to see it in your dog's face as well; check the snout to see if it is swollen, as well as the eyes. It often looks like your dog has been stung by a wasp. If your dog yips or howls when you touch his sensitive-looking snout, this is probably why. He may have trouble putting one or both of his back paws on the ground as his joints will become stiff and the legs may swell. Vomiting and diarrhea are also common when the disease starts to show.

Photo Courtesy of Jason and Bethany Justus

The disease usually presents at between 4 and 18 months in puppies, but it could show even earlier. There are no known cases of it showing for the first time in an adult.

If you see signs of the problem, get your puppy to the vet. You will be able to help keep your puppy cool by washing behind his ears and keeping him in a cool room. Changing his diet to a low-protein diet will help. Natural sulfur and fresh parsley can help to keep the symptoms from recurring.

Photo Courtesy
of Darrin Lum

Hip And Elbow Dysplasia

Hip and elbow dysplasia are common ailments for medium and larger sized dogs. Their diet (Chapter 12) as a puppy can help minimize the problem when they are adults. Both types of dysplasia are a result of the dog's hip and leg sockets being malformed and that often leads to arthritis as the improper fit damages cartilage. The condition is possible to detect by the time a dog becomes an adult (around 2 years old for the Shar-Pei). The only way to detect it is through X-rays.

This is a problem that your Shar-Pei may try to hide because he won't want to slow down. Your adult dog will walk a little more stiffly, or may pant even when it's not hot. The condition usually becomes more obvious as a dog nears his golden years. Similar to the way older people tend to change their gait to accommodate pain, your dog may do the same. Getting up may be a little more difficult in the beginning, and will likely get worse as he ages.

While surgery is an option in severe cases, most dogs can benefit from less invasive treatments:

- Anti-inflammatory medications – talk to your vet (dogs should not have large doses of anti-inflammatory drugs on a daily basis the way people do since aspirin and anti-inflammatories can damage your dog's kidneys)

- Lower the amount of high impact exercise your dog gets, especially on wood floors, tile, concrete, or other hard surfaces (given how much your dog probably loves to swim, you can move more to a swimming exercising regimen to keep him active without the jarring motions of walking on hard surfaces)

- Joint fluid modifiers

- Physical therapy

- Weight loss (for dogs who are overweight or obese)

Patellar Luxation

Shar-Pei may suffer from patellar luxation, which is also called slipping kneecaps. When the kneecaps are not properly fitted into the sockets, the back legs may have some minor problems. In most cases, patellar luxation is not a serious issue, and it is not known to cause much pain. However, occasionally it will require surgery to fix the repeated shift of the kneecap.

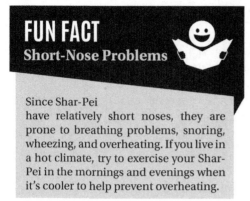

FUN FACT
Short-Nose Problems

Since Shar-Pei have relatively short noses, they are prone to breathing problems, snoring, wheezing, and overheating. If you live in a hot climate, try to exercise your Shar-Pei in the mornings and evenings when it's cooler to help prevent overheating.

If your Shar-Pei occasionally seems to be in pain when walking or cries when out running, this could be a sign of patellar luxation. Dogs tend to hold up the affected leg for a short period of time trying to relieve the pain. It can be difficult to detect unless a dog has a more severe case, particularly as your dog ages.

Hypothyroidism

This is a problem that is also found in humans (and many dog breeds). Hypothyroidism is a result of the person or dog not making enough thyroid hormone. It often begins to show in a Shar-Pei when he is between two and six years old, and symptoms include weight gain, lack of energy, and skin problems (such as dry or itchy skin).

A blood test is done to find out if a Shar-Pei has hypothyroidism. Some vets will conduct the test annually as a preventative measure. If your dog has hypothyroidism, your vet will likely prescribe an oral medication.

Eye Issues

All brachial dogs have eye issues because of the short length of their snouts. Shar-Pei do have issues, but they aren't as susceptible to them as many other brachial breeds. Still, you should know about the potential issues to make sure you properly take care of your pup's wise-looking eyes.

Entropion

Entropion is when the dog's eyelids roll inward, damaging the cornea as the eyelashes scratch it. The corrective surgery that fixes this problem can cause another eye disorder, ectropion. This is when the lower eyelid droops down so that you can see the soft pink tissue under the eye. While ectropion is not a serious problem – basset hounds live with it as a natural part of their facial structure – it does increase the likelihood of eye infections.

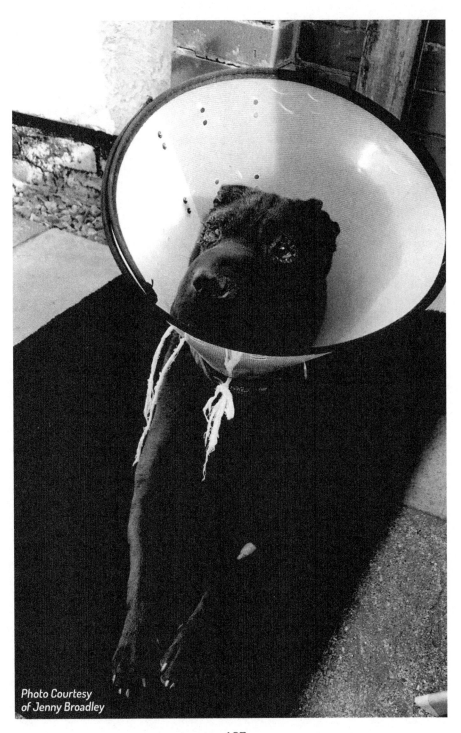

Photo Courtesy
of Jenny Broadley

Glaucoma

A painful eye ailment, glaucoma can result in blindness if it isn't treated early. If you notice your Shar-Pei's eyes watering a lot, the cornea turning blue, or your dog is squinting often, get him to the vet. These are signs that your dog is in pain, which can be difficult to notice because you get accustomed to the behavior.

You can also have your vet do an annual glaucoma screening. This will help you know that your dog is all right.

Progressive Retinal Atrophy (Pra)

Roughly 10% of Shar-Pei have PRA, which causes a sensitivity to light because of problems with the retina. Puppies should be tested, so if you adopt your puppy from a breeder, you should have a guarantee against this particular problem.

Dogs with this condition usually start presenting with night blindness, which can make your dog more nervous. If you look at your dog's eyes, they may also reflect light more as the eyes deteriorate. The ailment affects both eyes, so the problem should show in both.

There is no treatment for the condition. You will need to learn to accommodate your dog's failing sight over time.

Cherry Eye

Glandular hypertrophy, better known as cherry eye, is caused by the third eyelid becoming inflamed. When this happens, you will be able to see the eyelid as it distends outward. Although it looks horrible, the condition is easily treated through surgery.

Fungal Ear Infections

Dogs' ears can create a dark, warm place for fungus, yeast, and bacteria to thrive. With the Shar-Pei having ears that have a shorter vertical ear canal, there is a risk that your dog will develop ear infections. Allergies can be a major contributing factor, but all dogs are at risk for these types of infections. This is why it is absolutely essential that you do not let your dog's ears get wet during bath time, and why you must monitor his ear health. Watch for the following issues in your dog's ears:

- Colored discharge (particularly brown or bloody)
- Swelling and redness

- Crust forming on the skin of the ear flap

- Scratching at the ear or frequent shaking of the head

- Loss of hearing or balance

- Walking in circles (beyond the usual for bathroom inspections or nesting before lying down)

If you notice any of these symptoms, take your dog to the vet, even if the symptoms seem mild. There are a number of different available treatments, depending on the severity of the condition. Usually an antifungal cream will be recommended, but more serious problems (such as an infection in the middle ear) could require injections or surgery.

If your dog suffers from chronic fungal ear infections, your vet will likely recommend an ear cleaner designed to prevent the problem or a solution that will keep the area dry.

Tight Lip

Those unique jaws may cause problems with your dog's lips. When they have too much lower lip, it can cause the lip to roll over the lower teeth. Your Shar-Pei will definitely be bothered by this when trying to eat. The rolled lip can also push the teeth back. If this happens, surgery may be required to correct the issue.

Skin Problems

As noted before, your dog's wrinkles will require regular cleaning to keep them from getting infected. If you notice that your Shar-Pei has a rash (inflamed red areas that cause hair loss), it could mean that your Shar-Pei's skin is actually being irritated by his own coarse fur. There isn't much you can do since there is no effective treatment. It usually appears in patches, but occasionally can affect the entire body.

Common Owner Mistakes

In addition to genetic problems, there are things that you can do that could damage your dog's health related to diet and exercise levels. In the early days, it is a difficult balance to strike as your puppy is curious and enthusiastic. Even when he is a fully grown dog, you have to make sure

that you are minimizing how much stress is placed on your Shar-Pei's body. Weight management is one important way of keeping your dog healthy. You need to ensure that your dog is getting the right nutrition for his activity level to keep him from having a greater risk of exacerbating hip and elbow dysplasia.

Failing to notice early signs of potential issues can be detrimental, even fatal to your friend. If at any point you notice strange changes in your dog's behavior, take him to the vet. As a fairly healthy breed, strange behavior in a Shar-Pei is likely a sign of something that should be checked.

Prevention And Monitoring

The recent trend of "cute" overweight Shar-Pei has called attention to the potential health risks that this kind of trend can cause. This is a breed that is already cute, and you should never sacrifice your dog's health in the name of cute. Instead, take extra time to exercise with your dog. This is both healthier and more fun for your buddy and you.

Checking your Shar-Pei's weight is important and should be done at least once a quarter or twice a year. Your vet will likely talk to you if your dog is overweight because this not only puts a strain on the dog's back, legs, joints, and muscles, but it can also have adverse effects on your dog's heart, blood flow, and respiratory system. Make sure to talk to your vet if you notice that your Shar-Pei is having any trouble. Those regular vet visits can help you address issues that you may not think are that big a deal. Sometimes the symptoms you notice are a sign of a future problem.

CHAPTER 17
The Aging Shar-Pei

"Shar-Pei tend to gain weight as they get older. It is very important to keep them at their ideal weight to avoid joint pain. Older Shar-Pei (7 and older) should have yearly geriatric check ups and blood work."

Janet Saporito
Thornapple Hill Chinese Shar-Pei

Photo Courtesy
of Sara Beavington

The average life expectancy of a Shar-Pei is between 9 and 11 years old. If you take good care of your Shar-Pei, you will have a bit longer with your buddy. Of course it will never seem like it is enough time, but there is a lot you can do to extend your dog's life. A Shar-Pei that is well taken care of will live longer, which makes it all the more important to make sure your pup gets regular exercise and has a good diet.

Photo Courtesy of Kimberly Georgeff

At some point you will notice that your Shar-Pei is slowing down, and that is a sign that your friend is starting to feel the age in his bones. This usually happens at around 7 or 8 years old. A dog may remain healthy his whole life, but his body still won't be able to do the same activities as the years start to take their toll. The changes that are necessary as your dog ages will be based on your Shar-Pei's specific needs.

The first signs of age are usually your dog's walking becoming a little stiffer or when he starts panting more heavily earlier in the walk. If you see that, start to tone back the long walks, and just go for more, shorter walks. Your Shar-Pei may want to continue to be active, which means you will need to ensure the activity levels don't stop, just make an adjustment in the kinds of activities you do.

Your schedule is going to need to change as your canine slows down. Be careful to ensure that your pup doesn't overexert himself if he tries to remain active. Your Shar-Pei may not want to accept that things are changing and he won't be able to control it.

There is a reason these are called the golden years – you can really enjoy them with your dog. You don't have to worry as much about him tearing things up out of boredom or getting overexcited on walks anymore. You can enjoy lazy evenings and peaceful weekends with some less strenuous exercise to break up the day. It's easy to make the senior years incredibly enjoyable for your Shar-Pei and yourself by making the necessary adjustments.

Senior Care Challenges

In most cases, caring for an older dog is much simpler than taking care of a younger dog, and Shar-Pei are no exception. Accommodations you should make for your senior Shar-Pei include:

- Set water bowls out in a couple of different places so that your dog can easily reach them as needed.

- Cover hard floor surfaces (such as tile, hardwood, and vinyl). Use non-slip carpets or rugs.

- Add cushions and softer bedding for your Shar-Pei. This will make the surface more comfortable. There are bed warmers for dogs if your Shar-Pei displays achy joints or muscles often. Of course, you also need to make sure he isn't too warm, so this can be a fine balancing act.

- To improve his circulation, increase how often you brush your Shar-Pei.

- Stay inside in extreme heat and cold. An old canine cannot handle changes in temperature as well as he once did.

- Use stairs or ramps so that the old pup doesn't have to try to jump.

- Avoid moving your furniture around, particularly if your Shar-Pei shows signs of having trouble with his sight or has dementia. A familiar home is more comforting and less stressful as your pet ages. If your Shar-Pei isn't able to see as clearly as he once did, keeping the home familiar will make it easier for your dog to move around without getting hurt.

- If you have stairs that your Shar-Pei can no longer use, consider setting up an area where your dog can stay without having to go up and down the stairs too often.

- Create a space where your Shar-Pei can relax with fewer distractions and noises. Don't make your old friend feel isolated, but do give him a place to get away from everyone if he needs to be alone.

- Be prepared to let your dog out more often for restroom breaks.

Photo Courtesy of Rachael Walker

Common Physical Disorders Related To Aging

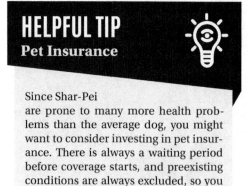

HELPFUL TIP
Pet Insurance

Since Shar-Pei are prone to many more health problems than the average dog, you might want to consider investing in pet insurance. There is always a waiting period before coverage starts, and preexisting conditions are always excluded, so you should get pet insurance as soon as you bring your Shar-Pei home.

Previous chapters cover illnesses that are common or likely with a Shar-Pei, but old age tends to bring a slew of ailments that aren't particular to any one breed. Here are other things you will need to watch for (as well as talking to your vet about them).

● Arthritis is probably the most common ailment in any dog breed, and the Shar-Pei is no exception. If your dog is showing signs of stiffness and pain after normal activities, talk with your vet about safe ways to help minimize the pain and discomfort of this common joint ailment.

● Gum disease is a common issue in older dogs as well, and you should be just as vigilant about brushing your dog's teeth when he gets older. A regular check of your Shar-Pei's teeth and gums can help ensure this does not become a problem.

● Loss of eyesight or blindness is relatively common in older dogs, just as it is in humans. Have your dog's vision checked at least once a year and more often if it is obvious that his eyesight is failing.

● Kidney disease is a common problem in older dogs, and one that you should monitor for the older your Shar-Pei gets. If your canine is drinking more often and having accidents regularly, get your Shar-Pei to the vet as soon as possible and have him checked for kidney disease.

● Diabetes is not as much of a risk for most of the dog's adult life. Although diabetes is usually thought of as a genetic condition, any Shar-Pei can become diabetic if not fed and exercised properly. This is another reason why it's so important to be careful with your Shar-Pei's diet and exercise levels.

Vet Visits

As your Shar-Pei ages, you are going to notice the slow-down, and the pain in your Shar-Pei's body will be obvious, just like it is in an older person. Make regular visits with your vet to ensure that you aren't doing anything that could potentially harm your Shar-Pei. If your Shar-Pei has a debilitating ailment or condition, you may want to discuss the options for ensuring a better quality of life for him, such as a wheelchair if your Shar-Pei's legs begin to have serious issues.

The Importance Of Regular Vet Visits And What To Expect

Just as humans go to visit the doctor more often as they age, you'll need to take your dog to see your vet with greater frequency. The vet can make sure that your Shar-Pei is staying active without overdoing it, and that there is no unnecessary stress on your older dog. If your canine has sustained an injury and hidden it from you, your vet is more likely to detect it.

Your vet can also make recommendations about activities and changes to your schedule based on your Shar-Pei's physical abilities and any changes in personality. For example, if your Shar-Pei is panting more now, it could be a sign of pain from stiffness. Your vet can help you determine the best way to keep your Shar-Pei happy and active during the later years.

The following are the kinds of things to expect when you go to the vet.

- Your vet is going to talk about your dog's history, even if you have visited every year. This talk is necessary to see how things have gone or if any possible problems have started to manifest themselves or have gotten worse.

- Your vet will probably conduct a complete physical examination to assess your dog's health.

- Depending on how old your dog is and the kind of health he is in, your vet may want to run different tests. The following are some of the most common tests for older dogs.

  - Arthropod-borne disease testing, which involves drawing blood and testing it for viral infections

  - Chemistry screening for kidney, liver, and sugar evaluation

  - Complete blood count

- Fecal Flotation, which involves mixing your dog's poop with a special liquid to test for worms and other parasites

- Heartworm testing

- Urinalysis, which tests your dog's urine to check the health of your dog's kidneys and urinary system

● The routine wellness check that the vet has been conducting on your dog for years

● Any breed-specific tests for your aging Shar-Pei

Changes To Watch For

Keep an eye out for different signs that your dog is slowing down. This will help you to know when to adjust the setup around your home and to reduce how much your old pup is exercising.

Appetite And Nutritional Requirements

With less exercise, your dog doesn't need as many calories, which means you need to adjust your pup's diet. If you opted to feed your Shar-Pei commercial dog food, make sure you change to a senior food. Senior food is designed for the changing dietary needs of older dogs, with fewer calories and more nutrients that the older dog's body needs.

If you make your Shar-Pei's food, talk to your vet and take the time to research how best to reduce calories without sacrificing taste. Your canine is going to need less fat in his food, so you may need to find something healthier that still has a lot of taste to supplement the types of foods you gave your Shar-Pei as a puppy or active adult dog.

Exercise

Despite the fact that your Shar-Pei may be independent, he will enjoy your attention as you exercise with him. If you make fewer demands, decrease the number of walks, or in any way change the routine, your senior Shar-Pei will quickly adapt to the new program. You will need to make those changes based on your dog's ability, so it's up to you to adjust the schedule and keep your Shar-Pei happily active. Shorter, more frequent walks should take care of your Shar-Pei's exercise needs, as well as helping to break up your day a little more.

Your dog will enjoy napping as much as walking, especially if he gets to cuddle with you. Sleeping beside you while you watch television or as you yourself nap is pretty much all it takes to make your older Shar-Pei content, but he still needs to exercise.

The way your Shar-Pei slows down will probably be the hardest part of watching him age. You may notice that your Shar-Pei spends more time sniffing during walks, which could be a sign that your dog is tiring. It could also be his way of acknowledging that the steady walks are a thing of the past and so he is stopping to enjoy the little things more. Stopping to smell things may now give him the excitement that he used to get by walking farther.

While you should be watching for your dog to tire, he may also let you know. If he is walking slower, looking up at you, and flopping down, that could be his way of letting you know it's time to return home. If your canine can't manage long walks any longer, make the walks shorter and more numerous and spend more time romping around your yard or home with your buddy.

Aging And The Senses

Just like people, dogs' senses weaken as they get older. They won't hear things as well as they used to, they won't see things as clearly, and their sense of smell will weaken.

The following are some of the signs that your dog is losing at least one of his senses.

- It becomes easy to surprise or startle your dog. You need to be careful because this can make your Shar-Pei aggressive, a scary prospect even in old age. Do NOT sneak up on your old dog as this can be bad for both of you, and he deserves better than to be scared.

- Your dog may seem to ignore you because he is less responsive when you issue a command. If you have not had a problem before, your dog isn't being stubborn, he is likely losing his hearing.

- Cloudy eyes may be a sign of loss of sight, though it does not mean that your dog is blind.

If your aging dog seems to be "behaving badly," it is a sign that he is aging, not that he doesn't care or wants to rebel. Do not punish your older dog.

Adjust your schedule to meet your dog's changing abilities. Adjust his water bowl's height, refrain from rearranging rooms, and pet your dog more often. Make sure that his bed is as fluffy as when you first got it, or get him a new bed. Put the bed on the ground if it was previously kept on furniture. Your dog is probably nervous about losing his abilities, so it is up to you to comfort him.

Photo Courtesy
of Christophe Bernard

Keeping Your Senior Dog Mentally Active

Just because your older Shar-Pei can't walk as far any longer doesn't mean that his brain isn't just as capable. In fact, the changes in his body will probably be frustrating for him, so you want to make sure he has plenty of other things to keep him active and happy. As he slows down physically, focus more on activities that are mentally stimulating. As long as your Shar-Pei has all of the basics down, you can teach him all kinds of low-impact tricks, if he likes to do tricks.

At this point, training could be easier because your Shar-Pei has learned to focus better and he'll be happy to have something he can still do with you. New toys are another great way to help keep your dog's mind active. Be careful that the toys aren't too rough on your dog's older jaw and teeth. Games such as hide and seek will still be very much appreciated. Whether you hide toys or yourself, this can be a game that keeps your Shar-Pei guessing. There are also food balls, puzzles, and other games that focus on cognitive abilities. A quick search online will turn up a wealth of different toys meant to help intelligent dogs to keep from getting bored.

For a dog like the Shar-Pei, additional attention and more petting will make him happy when he gets older. But you still want to make sure that your dog gets some physical and mental exercise regularly too. Even if your Shar-Pei's body has slowed down, his mind will tend to remain quite active.

Some senior dogs suffer from cognitive dysfunction (CCD) syndrome, a type of dementia. It is estimated that 85% of all cases of dementia in dogs go undiagnosed because of how difficult it is to pinpoint the problem. It manifests itself more as a problem of temperament.

If your dog begins to act differently, you should take him to the vet to see if he has CCD. While there really isn't any treatment for it, your vet can recommend things you can do to help your dog. Things like rearranging the furniture in your home are strongly discouraged as familiarity with his surroundings will help your dog feel more comfortable and will reduce stress as he loses his cognitive abilities. Mental stimulation will help to fight CCD, but you should plan to keep your dog mentally stimulated regardless of whether or not he exhibits symptoms of dementia.

Advantages To The Senior Years

The last years of your Shar-Pei's life can be just as enjoyable (if not more so) than the earlier stages since your dog has mellowed. All of those high-energy activities will give way to relaxation. Having your pup just enjoy your company can be incredibly nice (just remember to keep up with some of his activity levels instead of getting too complacent with your Shar-Pei's newfound love of resting and relaxing).

Your Shar-Pei will continue to be a loving companion, interacting with you at every opportunity – that does not change with age. Your canine's limitations should dictate interactions and activities. If you are busy, make sure you schedule time with your Shar-Pei to do things that are within those limitations. It is just as easy to make an older Shar-Pei happy as it is with a young one, and it is easier on you since relaxing is more essential to your old friend.

Preparing To Say Goodbye

This is something that no pet parent wants to think about, but as you watch your Shar-Pei slow down, you will know that your time with your sweet pup is coming to an end. Some dogs tend to suddenly decline, making it very obvious when you need to start taking extra care of their aging bodies. They have trouble on smoother surfaces or can't walk nearly as far as they once did. It's certainly sad, but when it starts to happen, you know it is time to begin to prepare to say goodbye.

Some dogs can continue to live for years after they begin to slow down, but many dogs don't make it more than about a year or two. Sometimes dogs will lose their interest in eating, will have a stroke, or other problem that arises with little warning. Eventually, it will be time to say goodbye, whether at home or at the vet's. You need to be prepared, and that is exactly why you should be making the most of these last few years.

Talk to your family about how you will care for your dog over the last few years or months of his life. Many dogs will be perfectly happy, despite their limited abilities. Some may begin to have problems controlling their bowel movements, while others may have problems getting up from a prone position. There are solutions to all of these problems. It is key to remember that quality of life should be the primary consideration, and since your dog cannot tell you how he feels, you will have to take cues from your dog. If your dog still seems happy, there is no reason to euthanize him.

At this stage, your dog is probably very happy just sleeping near you for 18 hours a day. That is perfectly fine as long as he still gets excited about walking, eating, and being petted. The purpose of euthanasia is to reduce suffering, not to make things more convenient for yourself. This is what makes the decision so difficult, but your dog's behavior should be a fairly good indicator of how he is feeling. Here are some other things to watch to help you evaluate your dog's quality of life:

- Appetite
- Drinking
- Urinating and defecation
- Pain (noted by excessive panting)
- Stress levels
- Desire to be active or with family (if your dog wants to be alone most of the time, that is usually a sign that he is trying to be alone for the end)

Talk to your vet if your dog has a serious illness to determine what the best path forward is. They can provide the best information on the quality of your dog's life and how long your dog is likely to live with the disease or ailment.

If your dog gets to the point when you know that he is no longer happy, he can't move around, or he has a fatal illness, it is probably time to say goodbye. This is a decision that should be made as a family, always putting the dog's needs and quality of life first. If you decide it is time to say goodbye, determine who will be present at the end.

Once at the vet's office, if you have decided to euthanize the dog, you can make the last few minutes very happy by feeding your dog the things that he couldn't eat before. Things like chocolate and grapes can put a smile on his face for the remaining time he has.

You can also have your dog euthanized at home. If you decide to request a vet to come to your home, be prepared for additional charges for the home visit. You also need to determine where you want your dog to be, whether inside or outside, and in which room if you decide to do it inside.

Make sure at least one person he knows well is present so that your dog is not alone during the last few minutes of his life. You don't want your dog to die surrounded by strangers. The process is fairly peaceful, but your dog will probably be a little stressed. He will pass within a few minutes of the injection. Continue to talk to him as his brain will continue to work even after his eyes close.

Once your dog is gone, you need to determine what to do with the body.

- Cremation is one of the most common ways of taking care of the body. You can get an urn or request a container to scatter your dog's ashes over his favorite places. Make sure you don't dump his ashes in places where that is not permitted. Private cremation is more expensive than communal cremation, but it means that the only ashes you get are from your dog. Communal creation occurs when several pets are cremated together.

- Burial is the easiest method if you have your pet euthanized at home, but you need to check your local regulations to ensure that you can bury your dog at home because this is illegal in some places. You also need to consider the soil. If your yard is rocky or sandy, that will create problems with trying to bury your pet at home. Also, don't bury your pet in your yard if it is near wells that people use as a drinking source, or if it is near wetlands or waterways. Your dog's body can contaminate the water as it decays. You can also look into a pet cemetery if there is one in your area.

Grief And Healing

Dogs become members of our families, so their passing can be incredibly difficult. People go through all of the same emotions and feelings of loss with a dog as they do with close friends and family. The absence of that presence in your life is jarring, especially with such a loving, loyal dog like the Shar-Pei. It will feel weird not to have that presence along behind you as you move around your home. Just as painful, your home is a constant reminder of the loss, and in the beginning you and your family will probably feel considerable grief. Saying goodbye is going to be difficult. Taking a couple of days off work is not a bad idea. While people who don't have dogs will say that your Shar-Pei was just a dog, you know better, and it is okay to feel the pain and to grieve like you would for any lost loved one.

Losing your Shar-Pei is also going to make a substantial change in your schedule. It will likely take a while to get accustomed to the way your day-to-day life has shifted. Fight the urge to go out and get a new dog because you almost certainly are not ready yet.

Everyone grieves differently, so you will need to allow yourself to grieve in a way that is healthy for you. Everyone in your family will feel the loss differently too, so let them feel it their own ways. Some people don't require much time, while others can feel the loss for months. There is no timetable, so don't try to force it on yourself or any member of your family. Talk about how you would like to remember your pup. You can have a memorial for your lost pet, tell stories, or plant a tree in your dog's memory.

Try to return to your normal routine as much as possible if you have other pets. This can be both painful and helpful as your other pets will still need you just as much (especially other dogs that have also lost their companion).

If you find that grief is hindering your ability to function normally, seek professional help. If needed, you can go online to find support groups in your area to help you and your family, especially if this was your first dog. Sometimes it helps to talk about the loss so that you can start to heal.

Photo Courtesy
of Claire Beaumont

Printed in Great Britain
by Amazon

41126174R00116